nature graphics

SendPoints

nature graphics

© SendPoints Publishing Co., Ltd.

EDITED & PUBLISHED BY SendPoints Publishing Co., Ltd.
PUBLISHER: Lin Gengli
PUBLISHING DIRECTOR: Lin Shijian
EDITORIAL DIRECTOR: Sundae Li
EXECUTIVE EDITOR: Ellyse Ho
ART DIRECTOR: Lin Shijian
EXECUTIVE ART EDITOR: Lin Shijian, Yu Kai, He Wanling
PROOFREADING: Faith Dexter, Sundae Li, Christina Hwang

ADDRESS: Room 15A Block 9 Tsui Chuk Garden, Wong Tai Sin, Kowloon, Hong Kong
TEL: +852-35832323 / **FAX:** +852-35832448
EMAIL: info@sendpoints.cn

DISTRIBUTED BY Guangzhou SendPoints Book Co., Ltd.
SALES MANAGER: Zhang Juan (China), Sissi (International)
GUANGZHOU: +86-20-89095121
BEIJING: +86-10-84139071
SHANGHAI: +86-21-63523469
EMAIL: overseas01@sendpoints.cn
WEBSITE: www.sendpoints.cn

ISBN 978-988-12943-3-3

All rights reserved. No part of this publication may be reproduced, stored in a retrieval system or transmitted in any form or by any means, electronic, mechanical, photocopying, recording or otherwise, without prior permission in writing from the publisher. For more information, please contact SendPoints Publishing Co., Ltd.
Printed and bound in China

THE COLORS OF NATURE

GRAPHIC MAKEOVER

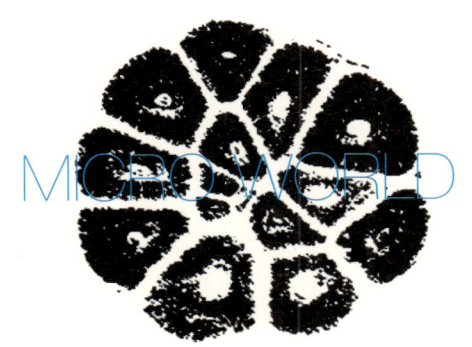

MICRO WORLD

Nature, the Fount of Inspiration

Nature is the home of amazing creatures, whose colors, shapes and structures never fail to give people a kick of inspiration which leads to extraordinary results. To designers in particular, nature is an inexhaustible fount of creative concepts. The trend of incorporating natural elements into design is inevitable due to a high demand for eco-sustainable development and the brisk advancement of visual media. Ingredients from creation may act as a motif, permeating an entire design, or as an inspirational background feature. Designers are influenced by various visual components of nature and proceed to trim them accordingly so as to infuse their design with vitality.

What is a natural element? It is the compilation of everything relating to nature, in every form. It is not limited to material elements such as organisms in the eco-system, but includes nonmaterial elements like the developmental process of nature. In short, natural elements are comprised of space and time, spirit and matter.

Natural elements are expressed two ways in design -- through figurative and abstract symbols. Figurative symbols show things as they actually appear through photography, realistic illustrations and the like -- duplicating the silhouette, color, texture, and pattern of the creature, whereas abstract symbols employ points, lines and surfaces to present the summarized, exaggerated, distorted or otherwise doctored version of colors, shapes and structures found in nature. Inspiration from nature is usually observed, extracted and expressed through various methods relying on the ingenuity of humanity.

Designers' primary ideas from nature stem from the field of textures. Colors can be treated in two ways in the design process: they can be visually duplicated and transposed or integrated within secondary designs.

MATERIAL
TEXTURE
SHAPE
COLOR
SHADE

However, nature has fewer textures to offer than it does patterns and colors. Natural patterns are a popular topic in the creation industry, especially in costume design, give boundaries and layers to otherwise plain designs. But, though natural textures and patterns are important, the hues therein are essential as well. These colors express the essential spirit of nature and give hints at the ruling principles behind Mother Nature to invent shades that do not exist in nature, which is a crucial step towards enriching an artist's palette. Until now, nature has been seen as a world of static objects, an obviously false perception as nothing remains stable. Fruits ripen and fall, water gushes and swirls, the moon waxes and wanes—and all this motion within nature causes our mental wheels to constantly gyrate as well. We have the laws of gravity, parabolic theories, thermodynamic laws…and so much more. These rules are an inseparable part of the enlightenment designers have gotten from the world. They are perhaps even more important than the previously-mentioned natural factors in deciding the aesthetics of design, since to create something which will appeal to human senses, the background dynamics applied to the elements are integral.

In the course of societal development, nature's contributions play a vital role with far-reaching impacts. As a means of survival, humans draw inspiration as well as resources from nature and modify it to improve their living conditions. Through their work, designers encourage us to rightly value our environment and establish harmonious relations between human beings. By wisely incorporating natural elements, design can raise awareness towards protecting both the eco-system and the human race.

© Onur Ertin

© Cody Petts

© Cody Petts

© Neue Design Studio

© Lin Shijian

© Lin Shijian

© Raffael Stüken

© David CHAMBON

© Onur Ertin

P8–P85

THE COLORS OF NATURE

P86–P191

GRAPHIC MAKEOVER

P192–P261

MICRO WORLD

NATURE GRAPHICS

The Colors of Nature

This big blue ball called earth encapsulates a mesmerizing world full of vivid colors. Nature's palette changes with the seasons, provoking diverse feelings: forest green evokes coziness, snowcap white suggests sorrow, rosy dawn arouses passion, dessert yellow hints of desperation, and sky blue emanates refreshment. We are used to associating colors with emotions, but there is also reason behind nature's distribution of color. Many animals evolve and alter their colors according to the environment they live in. Taking into consideration the sun, rain, temperature, geographical features, their predators etc., they develop an optimized shade for the purpose of hiding, baiting, or threatening. One of the most frequently cited examples is the chameleon, which can change its skin color in order to blend into the background to hide. Chameleon skin is an extreme example of the mysterious, yet sapient functionality of color in nature.

Every item in nature is bestowed with a hue of its own, and as earth's inhabitants, we are constantly stimulated by varying tints in different combinations and experience differing psychological effects from that stimulation. Color is the result of light reflecting off of the eyes' light receptors. The study of color - chromatics - focuses on how color influences the human psyche, known for its well-established branches of color psychology, color praxeology, bio-chromatics, and the geography of color.

Natural colors, as the origin of all other colors, aid the development and application of chromatics, effecting our behavior, perception and cognition. The dominance of color *in design - especially graphic design - is self-evident since it is the most direct form of visual stimulation. In this field color finds one its greatest outlet for expression. Imagine how desolate and boring the world would be without colors! Most designers pursue to discover a precise delegation of colors with which to suggest behavioral standards, evoke emotions, and communicate information.*

The world of colors is, in effect, an inexhaustible resource bank.

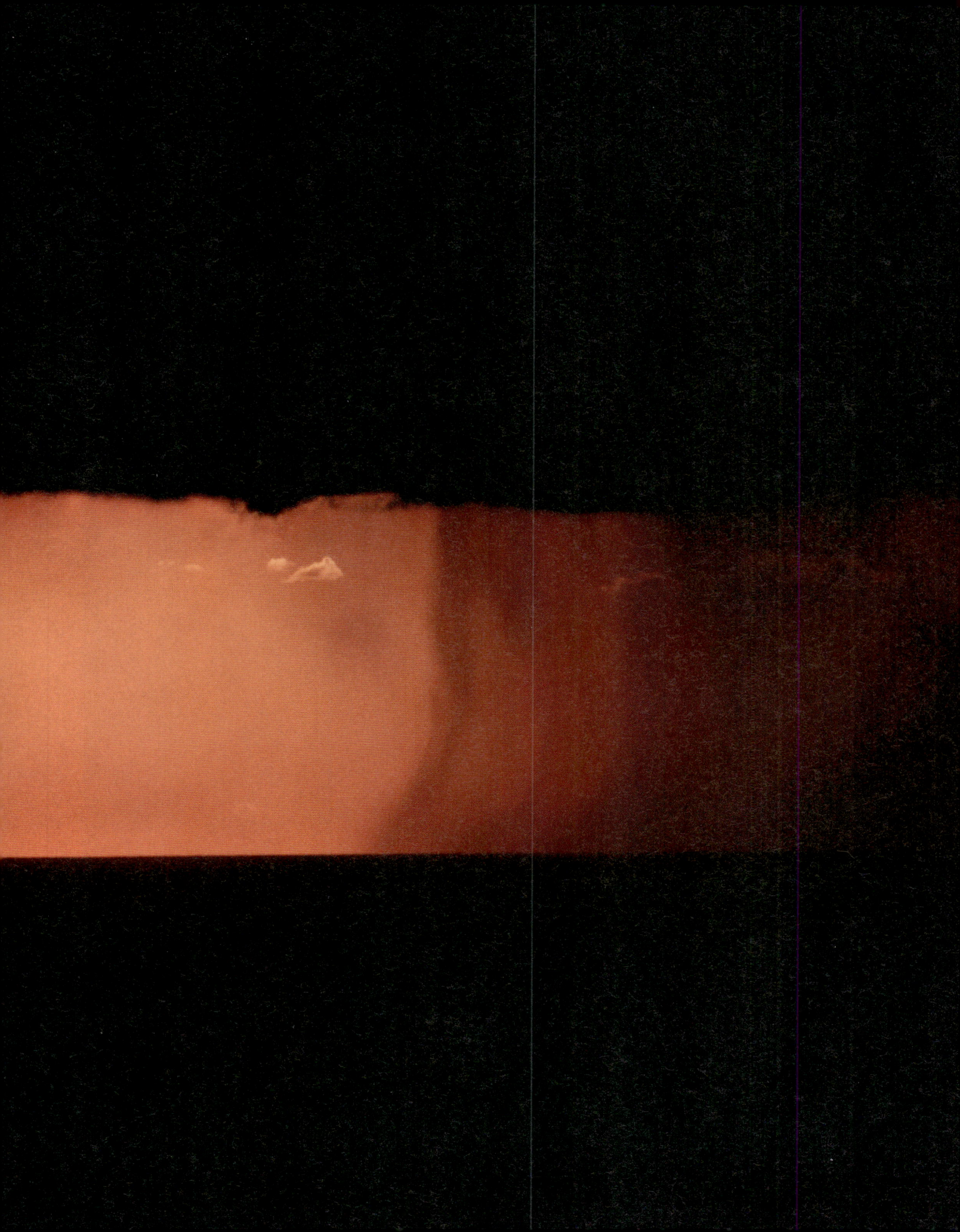

M.U.D

Short for "Making Upward Dance", M.U.D Centro Danza is a dance school in Italy. Highlighted in the school's identity are its two founders, Silvia and Leonardo. Their dancing postures fully express the contrast between serenity and tension and show to full effect the graceful impetus of two bodies.

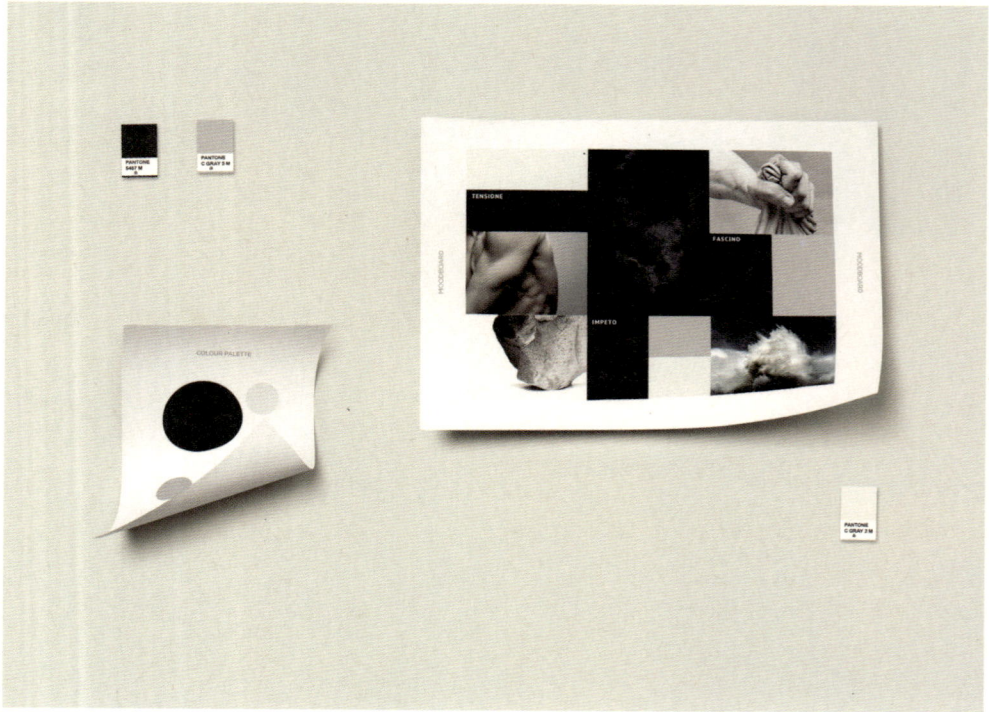

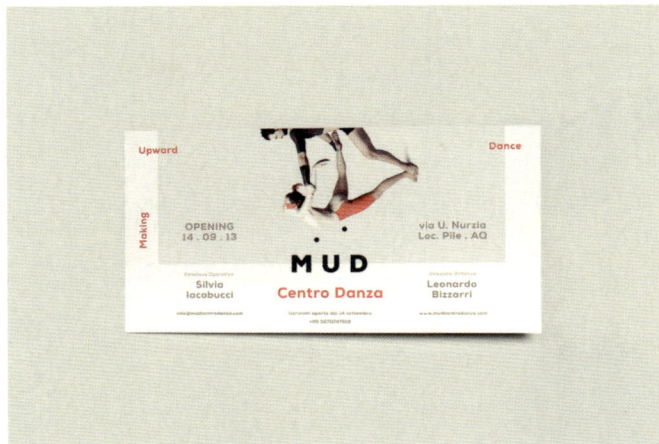

LE BLEURY

Le Bleury is a bar in Montreal near the Quartier des Spectacles. The bar's theme is based on the shape of a record. Its signature ends with a dash resembling a turntable. Event posters are made up of fragmented human bodies photographed in black and white and magnified flowers in pink, green and blue placed against a clinically clean background. The design combines an air of nostalgia with a modern flare through this dynamic approach.

DESIGN · Elizabeth Laferrière

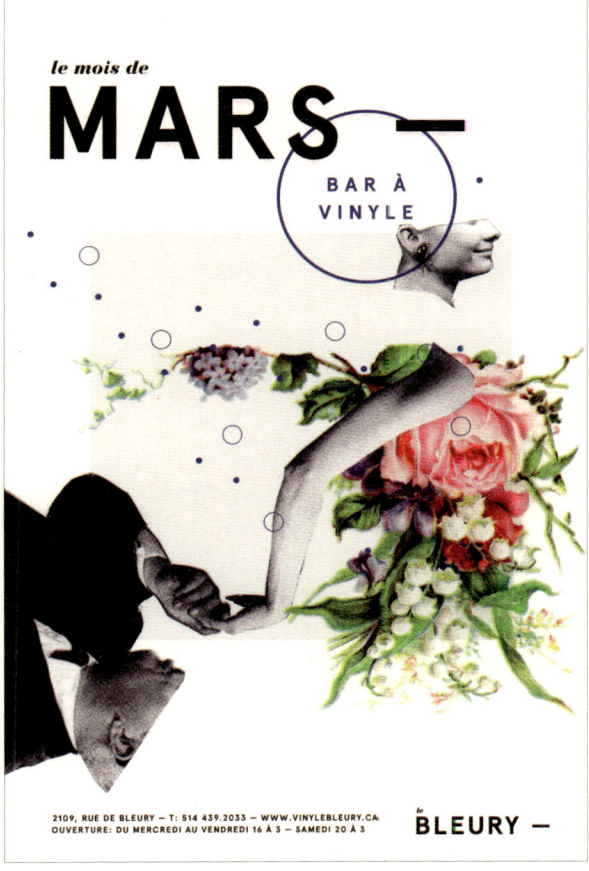

MISS KÕ

Miss Kõ is an underground Asian fusion restaurant located in the heart of Paris. Its logo was created using nine rice grains, because rice is the staple food in East Asia. The yakuza tattoos which include such oriental animal and plant patterns as carp and peony reveal its link to an Asian underworld and also expose Miss Kõ's rebellious characteristics.

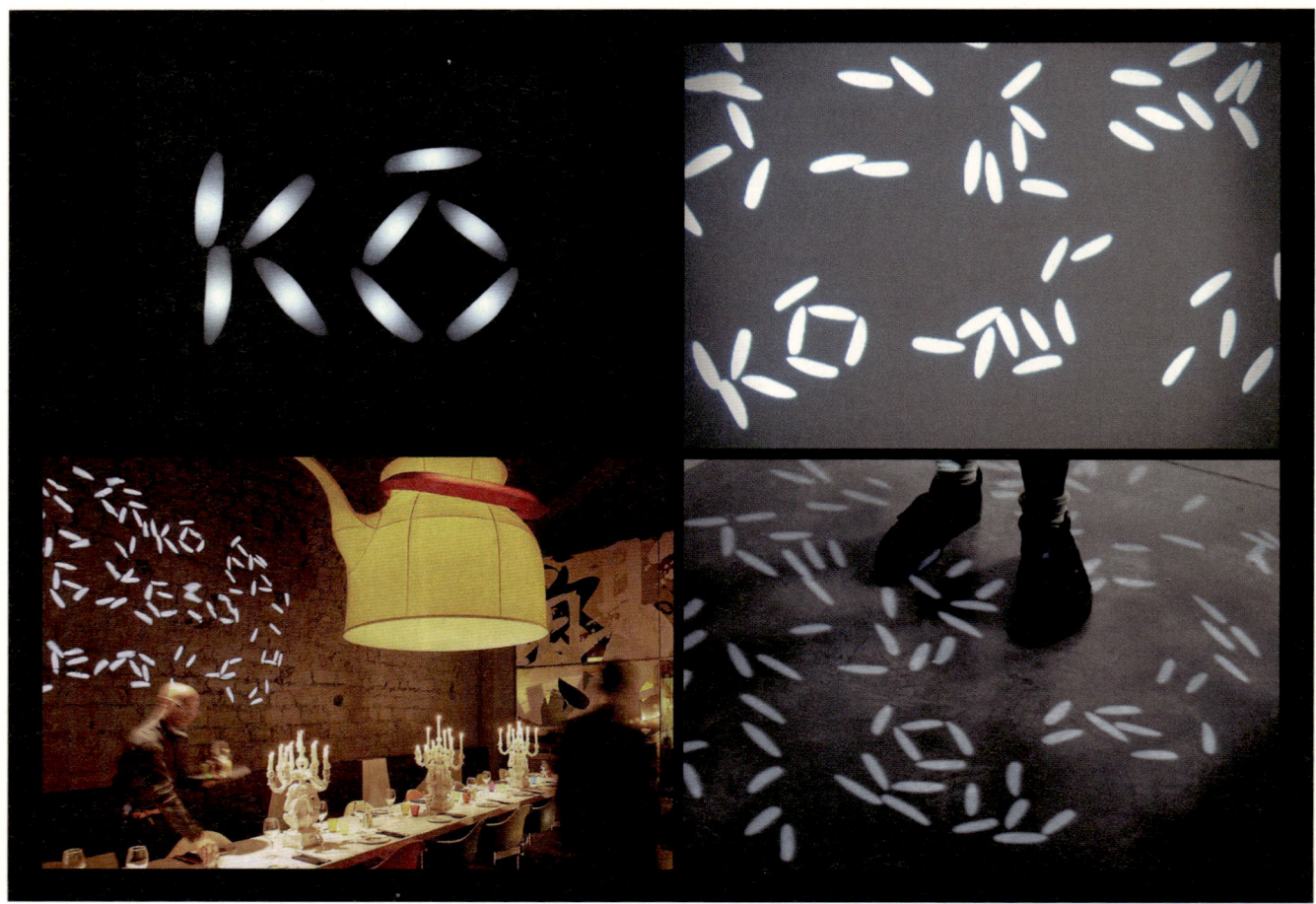

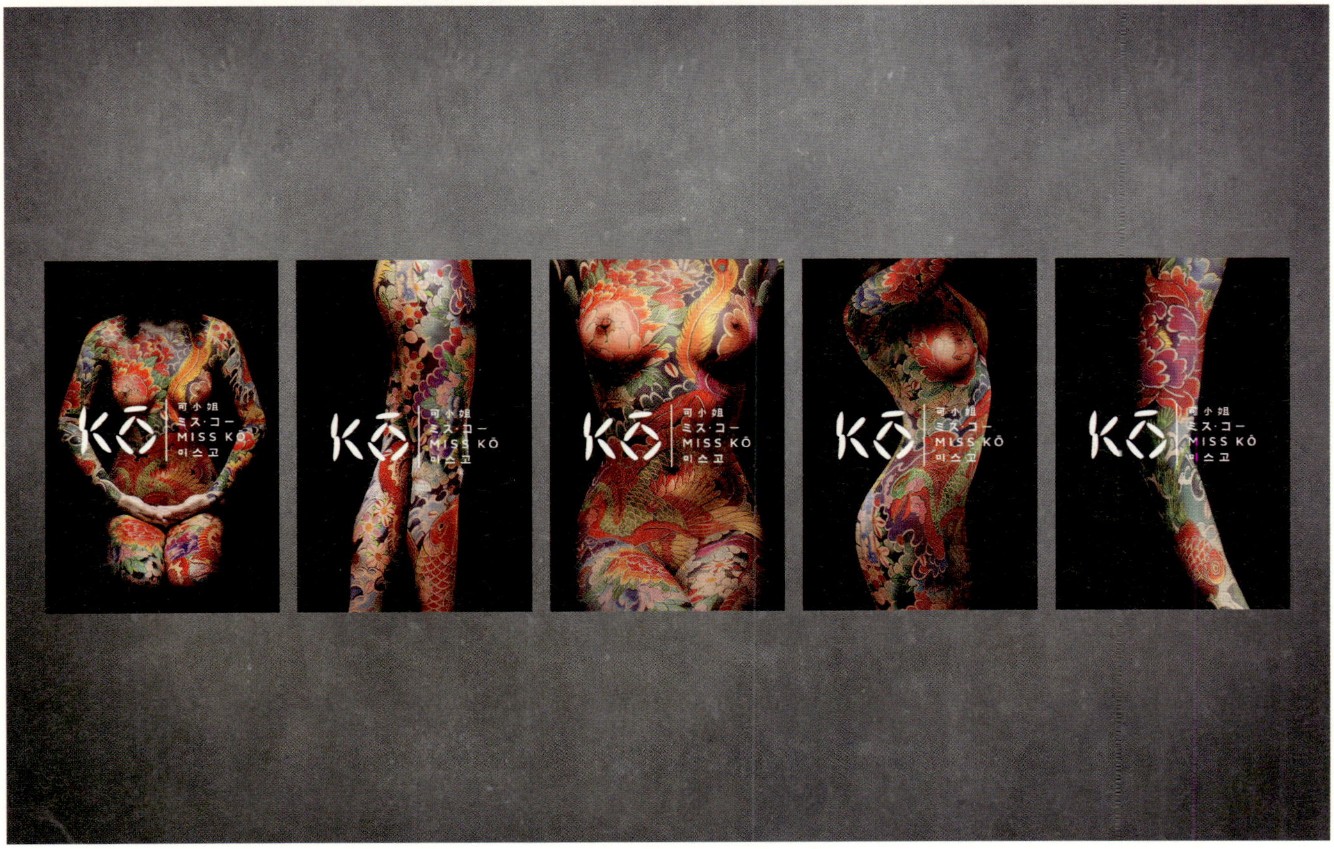

BUTTERFLY KINGDOM TAIWAN TEA

Packaging for a Taiwan tea brand is marked by a swarm of butterfly patterns. Drawn by colored pencils, the butterflies' textures, both delicate and plain, are completely and accurately expressed. Natural vitality is thus infused into the package, on which the "real" butterflies seems to be resting.

STUDIO · TROONION Design

DESIGN · Xie Yauzer

EPB

Gaining inspiration from nature through more artificial means, EPB made a fresh and energetic brand image of its own. Such a variety of floral patterns in bright and gorgeous colors clustered together could trigger a bout of hay fever.

EPB / Espacio Paco Bascuñán / Diseño & más   **EPB /** Espacio Paco Bascuñán / Diseño & más

EPB / Espacio Paco Bascuñán / Diseño & más   **EPB /** Espacio Paco Bascuñán / Diseño & más

HORTUS

The focal point for the brand design of a restaurant in Antwerp, Belgium consists of plant illustrations and a oval logo with saw blade. The smart use of various shades of green communicates the theme of a green paradise.

STUDIO · Ariadna Vilalta Creative Studio

DESIGN · Ariadna Vilalta

TAYLOR BLACK

Taylor Black is a brand of handmade jewelry in London. The rose+crown combination is the distinguishing feature of its logo. A sense of nostalgia is integrated into the brand identity by the use of Victorian plant illustrations which are vividly presented, generating a visual jolt.

FLINDERS HOTEL REBRANDING

Seesaw rebranded the Flinders Hotel located in the Mornington Peninsula. Designers used original collages in natural color schemes to create a series of delicate and unique patterns that encompass the Flinders Hotel's fine food selection, cultivating a fine, modern dining experience.

STUDIO · Seesaw

DESIGN · Matthew McKenzie, Anita Ryley

EXPLODED FLOWERS

Exploded Flowers is a series of artwork that presents common flowers from a completely unique perspective, creating an explosive visual effect, showing the intricate structures and aesthetic features of each petal, pistil and stamen.

DESIGN · FONG QI WEI

72 MAGIC POWER

In the identity for 72 Magic Power, gourds are arrayed in a variety of graphics such as zebra stripes, tiger skin, black and white grids, yellow dots against a blue background, etc. Thus the philosophy of "change" contributed greatly to this series of artwork.

DESIGN · Yu ZhiGuang

LUCIA

Lucia was inspired by the unforgettable memories of traditions past and by the clean, sensuous modernity of the future. The rare fragrant smells, beautiful colors and intriguing plant textures make these little wonders appear as precious perfumed jewels.

STUDIO · Pure Living

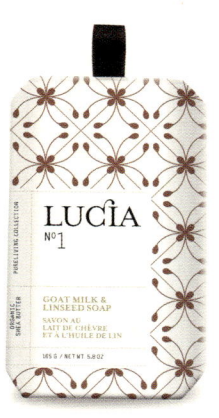

LIFE IS ENDLESS

Designers fashioned a skeleton from brightly-colored flowers and plants to illustrate that death embodies more than sorrow. This portrayal evokes warm feelings when you are seeing off a deceased loved one who is taking a journey to another world.

希望がある、死。
西日本典礼

BLUE HILL

Blue Hill co-owner and design director, Laureen Barber worked with Apartment One in branding and identity design to bring this savory yogurt line to life. They crafted vegetable illustrations and brushstroke lettering for each flavor. The warm hues of the illustrations and the cool slate stand strike just the right balance between authenticity and refinement.

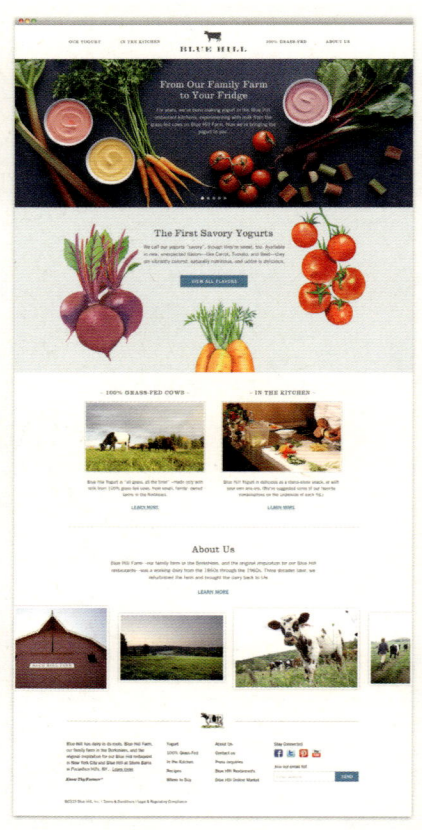

ITÁLIA ICE CREAM

Itália is a well-known ice cream brand in Rio de Janeiro. While redesigning their identity, designers retained the main characteristics of the old style. Local tropical elements are tastefully incorporated into the complicated patterns. Another highlight in the logo is the salmon-hued coconut tree device, small, yet exquisite.

STUDIO · DPZ Rio

DESIGN · Fernanda Schmidt, Arydéia Jardim Vianna

TREE RAIN WEAR

It is a piece of work for an art festival with the theme "Humans are part of nature". The design's aim to change people's melancholy impression of rain into a positive one. The rainwear can be folded and packed into a leaf-shaped bag.

STUDIO・MOTOMOTO INC.

DESIGN・Kenichi Matsumoto

MUNCHY SEEDS

Branding and identity for Munchy Seeds, a snack brand, is visually impressive because of the colorful animal images intricately painted on the hands. These varying gestures inject a natural dynamic into the brand.

STUDIO · Ziggurat Brands

DESIGN · Andy audsley

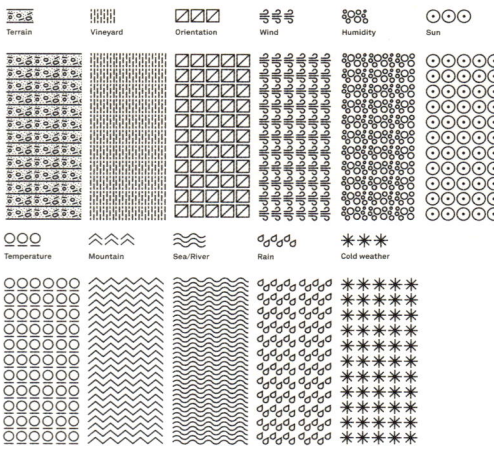

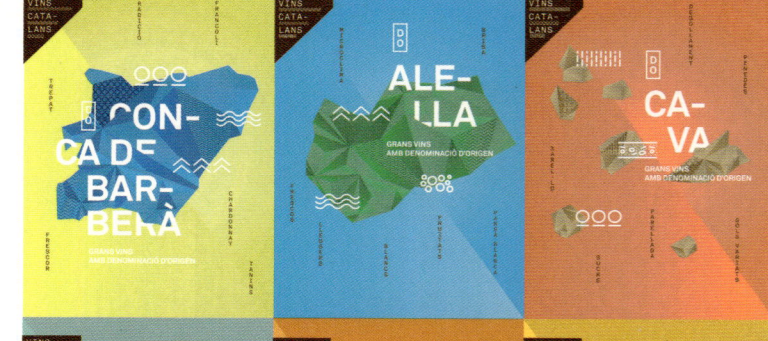

CATALAN WINES

Branding and identity for a Catalan wine is ornamented with geometric patterns in contrasting cool and warm hues that resemble topographic maps? of the territory. Waves, chevron lines and other graphics, acting as local weather indicators help to illustrate Catalan's identity.

STUDIO · toormix

DESIGN · Ferran Mitjans, Oriol Armengou, Gerard Marín

B HONEY CACHAÇA

B Honey Cachaça is a newly-developed liquor brand. Packaging design is featured in yellow and black stripes, taking on the semblance of a bee. A simple black logo is reminiscent of both a bee and a drop of honey. The "B" letter contains an exaggerated serif that looks like a stinger.

STUDIO · Pereira & O'Dell

DESIGN · Raimundo Favacho, Patricia Ebner

A BOTTLE TO BE PEELED

To launch a new formula of flavors of the world-renown Brazilian drink, Smirnoff Caipiroska, designers clad the bottles with sleek paper bearing the texture of fruits such as lemons, passion fruits and berries. Thus consumers are afforded the unique experience of peeling a drink bottle.

STUDIO · JWT BRAZIL

DESIGN · Mario D'Andrea, Roberto Fernandez

SYNDICATE ORIGINAL

Collaborating with well-known artists and illustrators, designers have treated street style in a unique and fresh way. Inspired by American heritage, and by the simplicity and minimalism of Scandinavian aesthetics, and also as a result of multicultural fusion, a comfortable feel was brought about with a select natural palette.

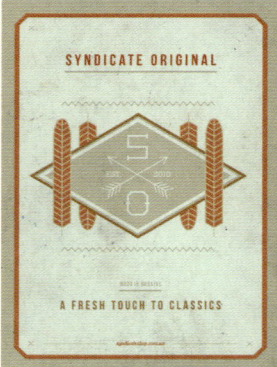

STUDIO · Orka Collective

DESIGN · Anton Abo, Ooli Mos

ATELIER FOOD

Atelier Food is a project that seeks new solutions in dealing with food. On the white grid background are colorful cooking materials of various sizes and forms arranged into a model of a city. This still-life image reflects the relationship between food and society.

VIVANA

Vivana is a Mexican brand of highly nutritious food products made from natural ingredients and antioxidants. Simple and concrete graphic language (that is, the patterns of ingredients) was applied in the logo and packaging, so as to highlight the brand's natural and purifying properties. In addition, the product description lies on the upper portion of the packaging, making it easier to be read.

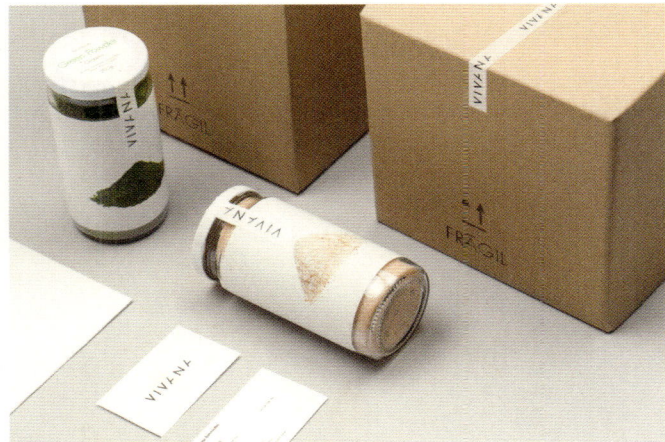

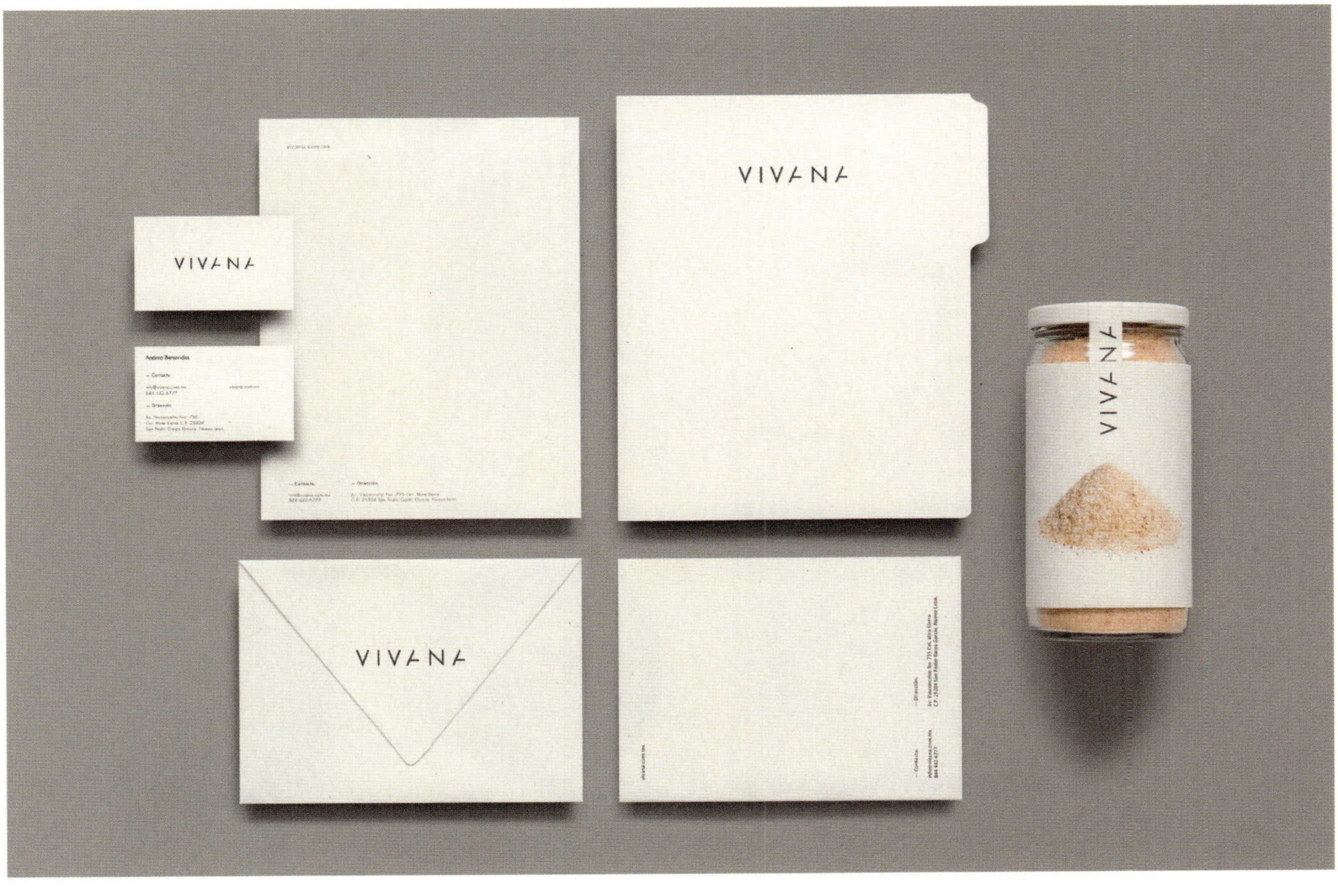

STUDIO · Anagrama

GREEN LAB

Green LAB is a restaurant, laboratory, and a shop. Vegetables, fruits, and herbs are grown at the restaurant and customers can choose the ingredients for their dish themselves. The identity design is based on green dots. The grid symbolizes order. Each dot is unique and of irregular shape which shows that they are not man-made but created by nature.

DESIGN · Diana Gibadulina

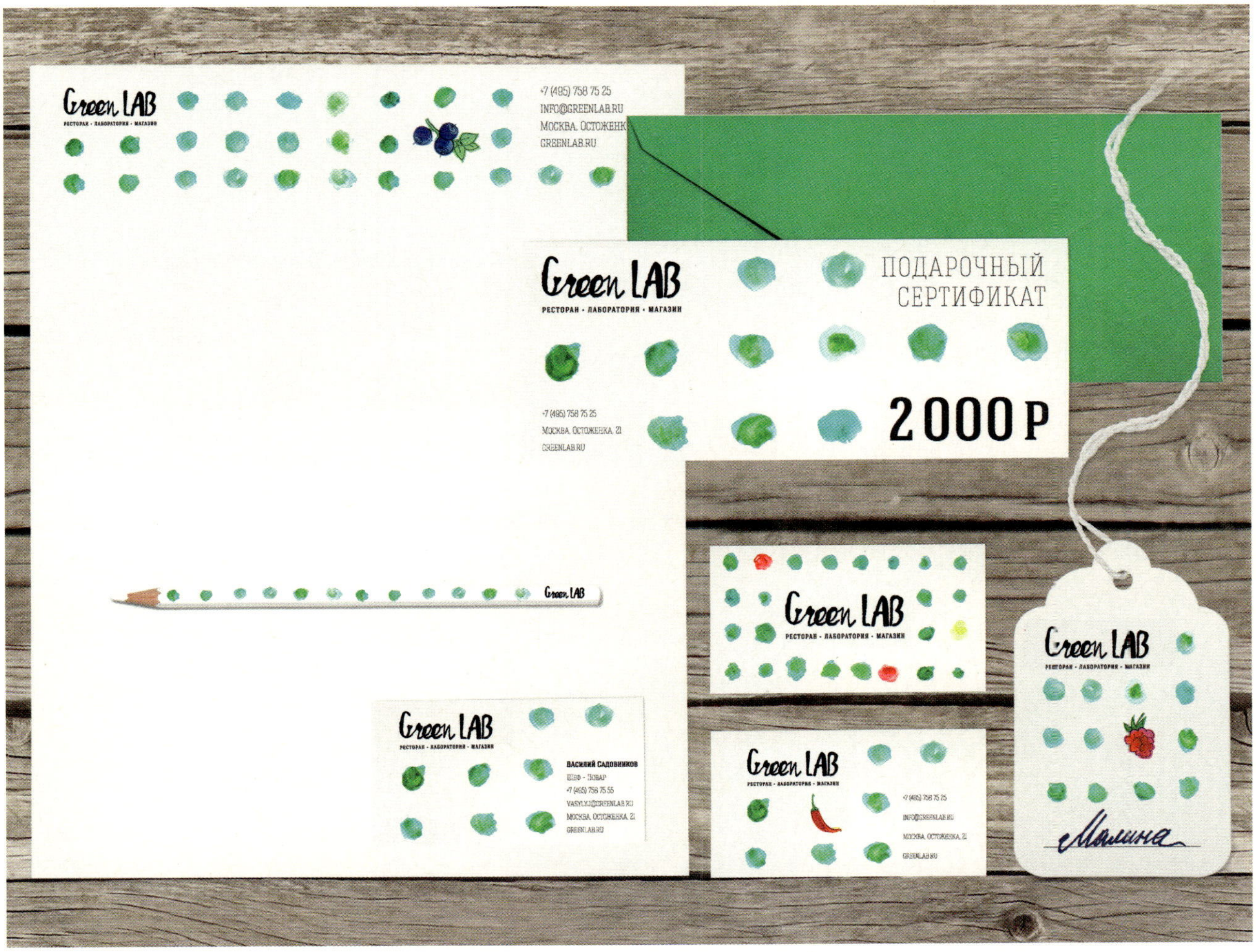

COLOR CARDS - PHOTOGRAPHY

In a visual research on cross sections of various vegetables graphics are put together to generate new patterns and artistic tensions.

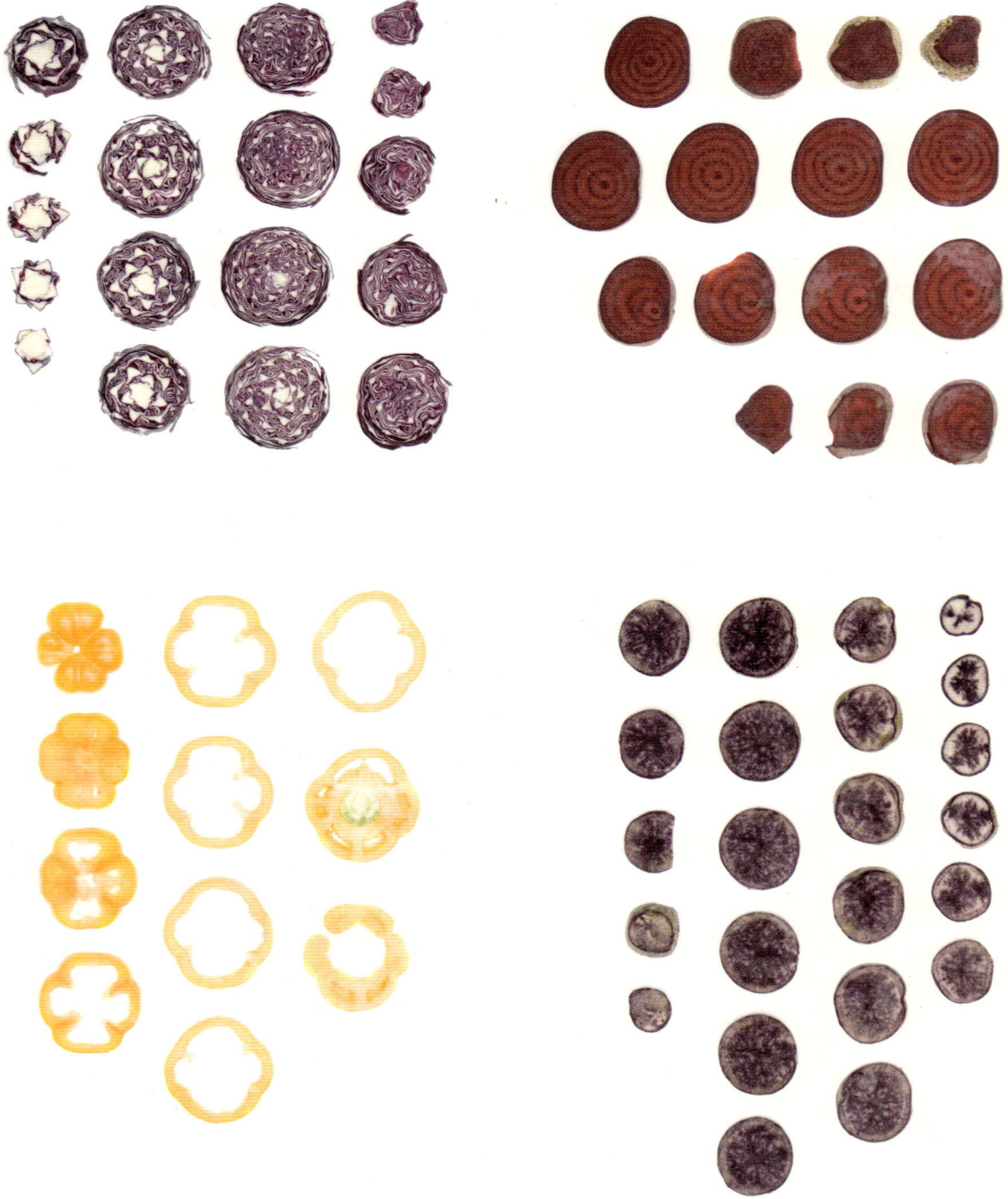

LUNG FESTIWAL

The LUNG festival is an art and culture festival held in Iceland, which is depicted as "the lung of Europe" in the design. The design consists of a symbol, which is the contour of the island, and typographic characters naming the event. The water surrounding Iceland, as well as the glaciers and falls throughout the country, inspire its dark turquoise color. Ruby red tones radiate the vivid undertones of molten lava. "Simple" and "clean-cut" are two key words to describe this design.

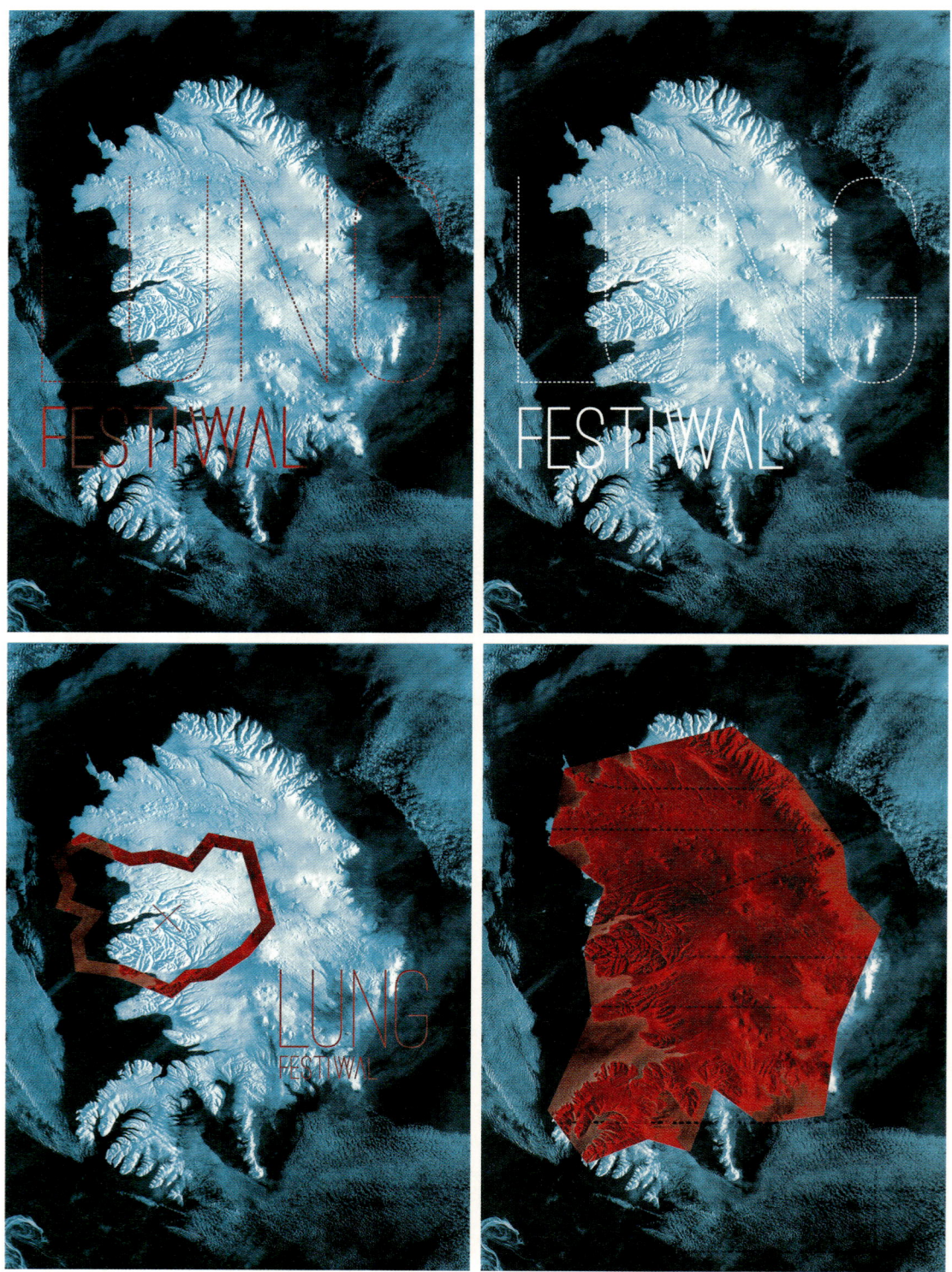

PODI

Podi, a new all-day restaurant that celebrates bold, robust and unique flavours takes on an equally bold and straightforward branding and identity. Derived from the meaning of Podi in Hindi - a coarse mixture of ground dry spices and herbs, a simple and modern logo with a strong hue was developed. The earthy tones reflect Podi's mission of making good, natural and organic food.

COLOUR

PODI
THE FOOD ORCHARD

STUDIO · Bravo Company

DESIGN · Jasmine Lee

ACRE

ACRE is a creative agency that provides innovative solutions for business problems. Yellow was chosen as the color of its identity to symbolize it as a harvest collaborated by designers, the clients and partners.

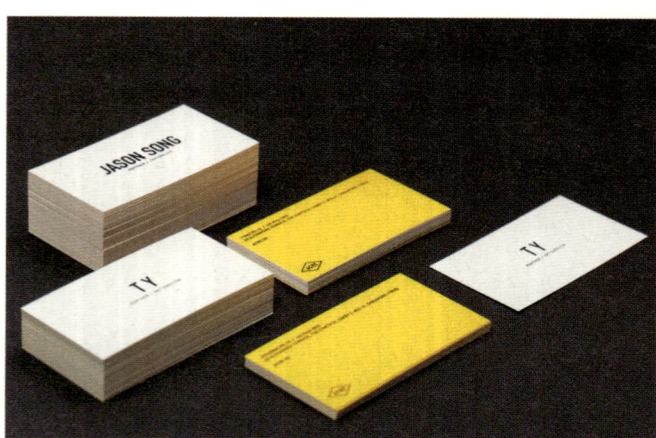

CALENDAR 2013

Calendar design inspired by the beauty of seasonal plants. The sumptuous photographs dance with the rhythmic typography, leading your thoughts to the best moments of every season.

PHOTOGRAPHER · Dagna Napierala

CYNAR ARGENTINA

This is the identity designed for Cynar, a well-known Italian alcohol brand based in Argentina. The logo was inspired by the artichoke. Designers used several different colors to attract younger audience.

STUDIO · MAMBO art&design studio

DESIGN · Martina Carcavallo, Damian Rozina

SKYLIGHT FARM

Skylight Farm at Skip's Garden is an organic vegetable farm located outside of Atlanta. Vintage farm labels and original hand-drawn illustrations of vegetables and farm equipment inspired the brand's identity.

SALE IN ZUCCA

Sale in Zucca is an event in which the pumpkin is the fil rouge. Colors used in the design are warm and have a taste of wet earth. Sale in Zucca is an Italian expression that means "be smart". It is a weekly appointment in one of the havens of the Tyrrhenian Sea, La Casetta (Terracina). The home-made quality of the identity emphasizes the attention of organic, natural and traditional food.

NATURE GRAPHICS

Graphic Makeover

It is not beauty that is lacking in the world, but the eyes to perceive it and the wisdom to capture it that are scarce.

Our beautiful blue planet is blessed with a diverse ecosystem, where the sky, ocean, land, air, rock, forest, rain and vegetation sustain the human race and help to promote the development of civilization. Humankind obtains its knowledge of the world from nature and its Creator: whether through science and technology or art and culture, knowledge is ripe for the picking from the exploration and cognition of our environment. Ancient civilizations worshipped nature due to their limited understanding of the world, but with new scientific discoveries man has learned to alter natural resources for his own use, even transcending the bounds of earth to investigate outer space. This journey exhibits the codependent relationship between the development of human society and nature.

Nature, the foundation of our existence, is also the inspiration for social advancement. During the progress, art and culture have equipped us with the unique ability to transform experiences and history into a massive hoard of visualized records, which have greatly promoted posterity.

Many remarkable works of art such as ancient murals, traditional Chinese freehand paintings, Japanese Ukiyo-e, conventional Egyptian paintings (in which the figure's head, chest, and legs are shown in profile, the eyes and the shoulders viewed from the front, and the waist and hips displayed in three-quarter view), realistic paintings of the Renaissance period, Impressionistic works, Constructivism and Abstract Expressionism, are credit to the experimental attempts and innovative presentations of what was perceived from the observation and assimilation of nature. These ingenious representations of different artistic styles are no doubt treasures of civilization, and will certainly impact the direction of the development of contemporary art and aesthetic standards.

Owing to the unambiguous nature of an image and the intense psychological suggestions provoked by visual simulation, the function of a picture has extended from an expression of art and culture or a means of recording to an efficacious medium for information transmission.

Contemporary images with their numerous channels of presentation and the constant demand for diversity, tend to become an all-inclusive reflection of regional culture, psychological projection, aesthetic standards, visual pleasure, market demands, social demands etc.

The aforementioned facts ought to be taken into account when designers attempt to create an image or visualize information. Inspiration can be derived from our understanding of the world, aesthetic accomplishment, cultural impact, or personal hobbies, but generally the most important factors can be traced to the wonders of this beautiful blue planet that nourishes us.

All perceivable colors and shapes are ripe to inspire us to change and reinvent this world. Life is filled with revelations and wonder, which will one day be conveyed to our daily lives through wisdom and culture.

PINE TYPEFACE

"Pine" is a finely crafted typeface embodying the strength and elegance of nature. Laser-cut from wood, each character emanates rich physicality while maintaining graphic sophistication.

MOUNTAIN

"BEEN FEARSOM CONFUSED FOR A MONTH OR TWO, BUT NEVER BEEN LOST."

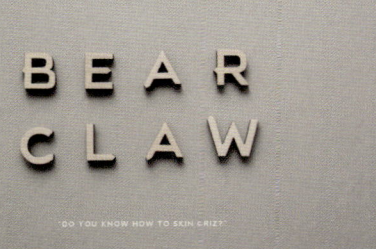

BEAR CLAW

"DO YOU KNOW HOW TO SKIN GRIZ?"

RIVER

"YOU CANNOT STEP INTO THE SAME RIVER TWICE."

DEL GUE

"I WEREN'T MORMONS, A CHIEF, HAND OF MAD WOLF. NICE FOLKS."

WILD

"THE CORE OF MANS' SPIRIT COMES FROM NEW EXPERIENCES."

ARCTIC AND ANTARCTIC MUSEUM

A comprehensive identity has been built for one of the major museums of St. Petersburg. The logo, made up of three triangles, was inspired by elements in the Arctic and Antarctic such as the polar bear, penguin, glacier and adventurer which are exhibited in the museum. The palette of the project is an honest record of natural colors found around the two areas: aquamarine, mulberry and cool blue. A set of complicated patterns harmoniously groups the marine creatures mentioned above.

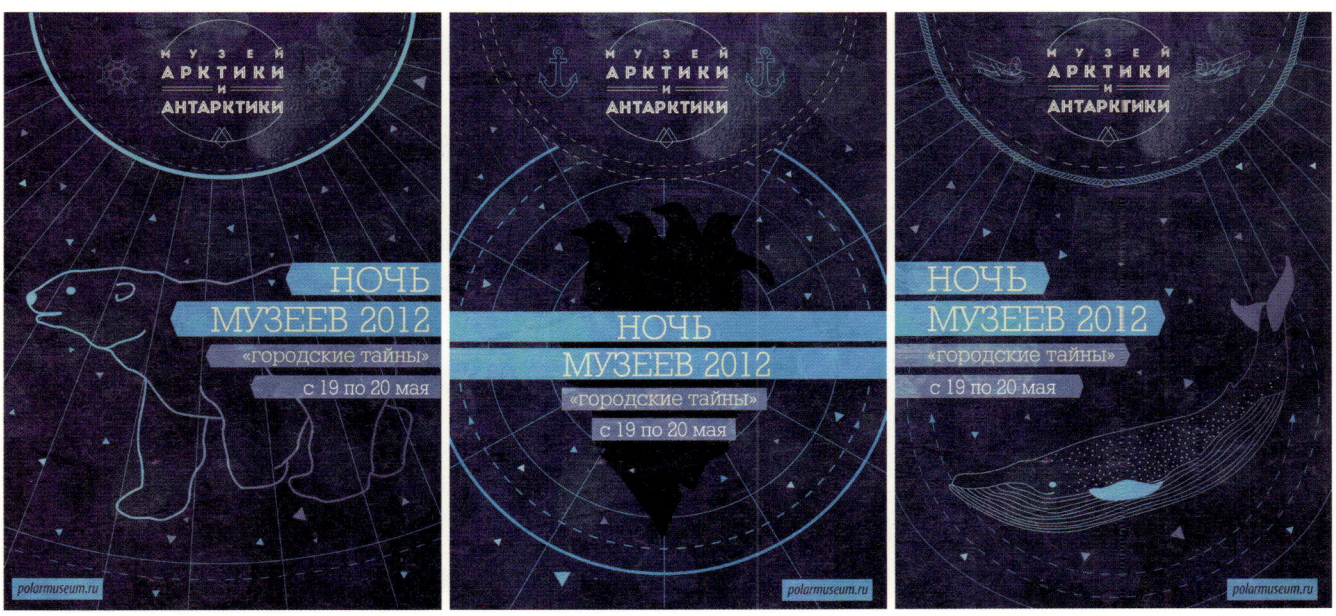

DESIGN · Yana Basirova

1. Grazie! 2. 紙醉金迷 3. 國王的新衣 4. Take My Hand
5. Eternal Embrace 6. 未婚妻的祕密 7. 班比去旅行 8. Buxton Love
9. Aphrodite 10. Golden Horns 11. 熟睡的美人魚

THE WILD RABBIT

The logo consists of a rabbit and a custom typeface inspired by nature and tree branches. The identity communicates the free spirit of a thriving boutique that revives and repurposes vintage jewelry from around the world.

| **New In Store!** | 11/26/2012　經典白特輯 | |

1. 索愛　　2. 月光小夜曲　　3. 羅馬之戀　　4. Hello Autumn
5. 無垠白畫　　6. 奶油波蘿　　7. Bon Voyage　　8. Infinity
9. 夢幻曲　　10. Hansel & Gretel　　11. 巴黎小塔　　12. 深雪冬眠

Grand Opening

FREE SHIPPING!

開幕慶!
活動期間免運費

10/22 - 10/31

about 小野兔:
傳達輕古感的生活態度,
為古董寶藏物歸原主.

find us:
facebook.com/
followthewildrabbit

ZEN

Packaging for ZEN perfume is a terrific marriage of natural-object like forms and glass bottles. Shapes of bamboo, shell and stone infuse the spirit of nature into the perfume bottles, fully realizing the ideal of Zen-calmness and contemplation.

LINNAEA

The design is a modern-day, slightly twisted interpretation of "Rhizotomi", an ancient character with knowledge of plant-life, nature and the workings of the universe. It's also linked to the founders' background in medical anthropology and plant biochemistry.

RICE GARDEN

This project was inspired by a Taiwanese saying: a dish cannot be good without a better bowl of rice. The intimate relationship between rice and the dishes it is served with is depicted in the calendar as seasonal vegetables in different months collaged with the image of rice.

STUDIO · Victor Branding Design Corp

DESIGN · Xu Guiping

THE SECRET GARDEN

The Secret Garden is a traditional bed & breakfast in Cape Cod, America that has been around for generations. Thus it was important to develop a brand that was fresh & contemporary to attract a new generation of guests, but also keep its fair for quaint charm and nostalgia in tact.

THE SECRET GARDEN
INN BY THE SEA • PROVINCETOWN • CAPE COD

STUDIO · Booth

DESIGN · Christian, Allegra Poschmann

EL MONTERO

El Montero is a restaurant located in the desert region of northern Mexico, the surroundings of which are reflected in its settings. Inspired by local food, the menu combines modern cooking utensil elements. The designer has widely incorporated native natural objects into his work, creating the concept of "delicious food throughout the district".

ANGUS 6

Angus 6 is a premium beef brand that sells only Australian beef. The concept behind this brand is "The Great Inheritance," emphasizing the great nature of Australia. The designers gave exquisite brand look by the use of strong contrasting black and white color palette mingled with beefy red. The traditional serif font (both English and Korean) adds authentic appearance to the brand as well.

STUDIO : EGGPLANT FACTORY

DESIGN : BOBAE KIM, YOUNGJI JUNG

ELK FABRIQUE PUB

This is the logo design and corporate identity for E.F. Pub. As the basic element of the design is a deer-shaped logo with the name of the pub embedded in it. Another notable feature is a deer head as well as a fork and slotted shovel are applied in assorted patterns.

A deer head is an alternative element of corporate identity, which is used in the design of documents folder and different advertising media.

DESIGN · Anton Starodubtcev

XUBEROA

This picture depicts the branding and identity for Xuberoa - a farm school offering primary education where various farm animals coexist in a sustainable natural environment. The logo is a cat-shaped design put together by a tangram. Other tangram-constructed animal patterns such as a dog, a pig, and a rooster are also applied in the identity. These elements endow the design with a fresh feel of nature.

BASERRI ESKOLA

STUDIO · stsdg

DESIGN · Jesús Sotés Vicente

XIN YUE

Identity and branding for Xinyue Business Club is marked by Chinese cultural elements. The logo is a circle with flowers, twigs and leaves within structured to form the Chinese character "Yue (namely 'to cross over')". Magpies perching on the twigs serve as an auspicious sign while the pure, elegant palette lends an artistic feel to the sophisticated pattern.

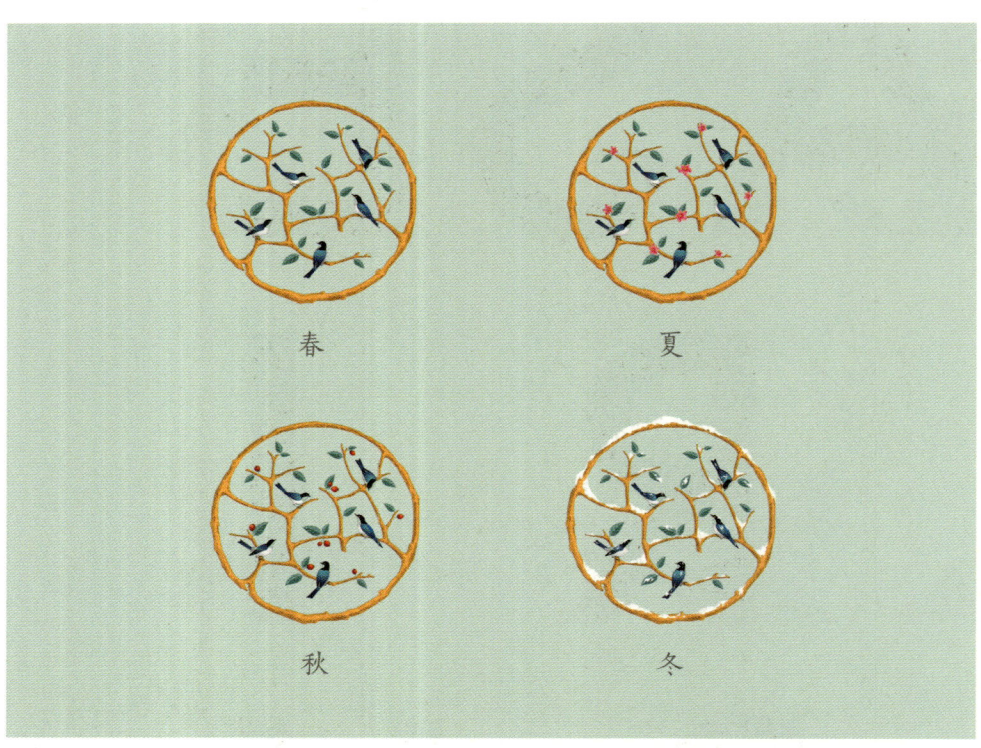

DESIGN · Peng Chao

JEONJU INTERNATIONAL FILM FESTIVAL

JIFF (Jeonju International Film Festival) is one of the three leading film festivals in Korea, which takes place every spring. Butterfly wings were used as the festival's motif in the 2013 season. The new identity design employed flapping butterfly wings as a design factor and blossoming flowers for the color structure. Endlessly flapping wings express the perseverance of filmmakers. More importantly, the design exemplifies the festival's spirit - small steps bring a big change.

Logo Basic

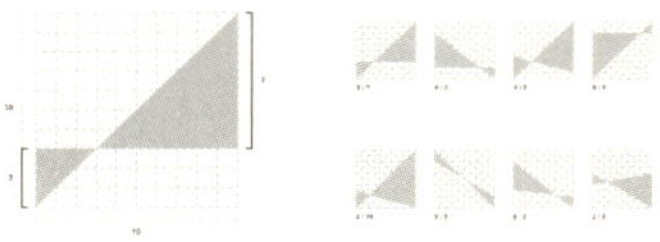

Signature

KARMA SUSHI

For Karma Sushi's, a Danish chain of sushi stores, a logo was born out of the image of a fish, reflecting the philosophy of karma. Sushi-related materials such as the meat of salmon and grey stone inspired the palette.

MADAM SIXTY ATE

Designers used journal entries within menus and a series of paintings that intermingled animals with vegetables to emphasize the whimsical, eccentric nature of the restaurant and its unusual pairings of food.

    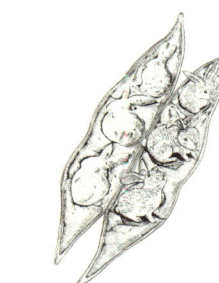

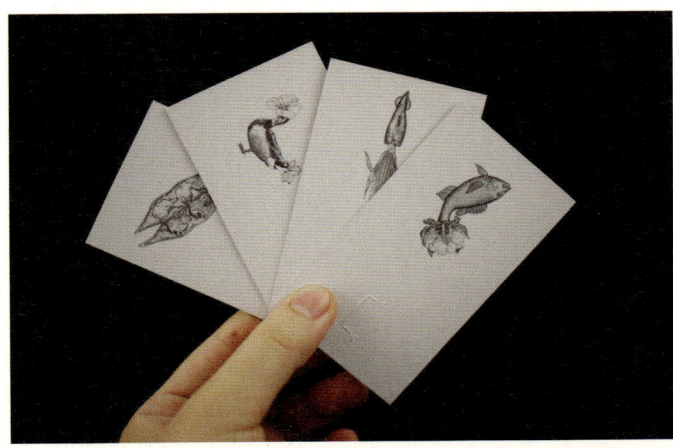 

STUDIO · Substance Limited

DESIGN · Jeremy Heun, Mandy Chan

A-MOLOKO

The design concept of the logo was inspired by the chain's business - automated sale of farm-fresh milk and the company's name, A-moloko, which was developed as well. The first letter, "A", which when turned upside-down resembles the muzzle of a cow, becomes the basis of the logo. The visual identity is built on a clear system of symbols, which follows the path of the milk from the cow to the consumer.

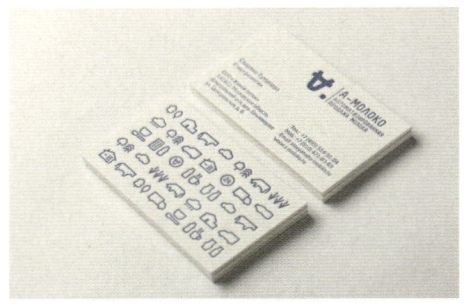

STUDIO · Ermolaev Bureau

DESIGN · Vlad Ermolaev

BIOPARCO DI ROMA

Bioparco di Roma is a zoological garden established in Rome. The park's corporate identity, features a modern look matching the design of the most famous tourist location in the city. In order to represent the free and happy character of animals and expose the scientific aims of the garden, the designer picked out a native totem as a logo. It has deep meaning, with recognizable animal elements. Founded on his research, the designer created an accessible, clear, and simple identity.

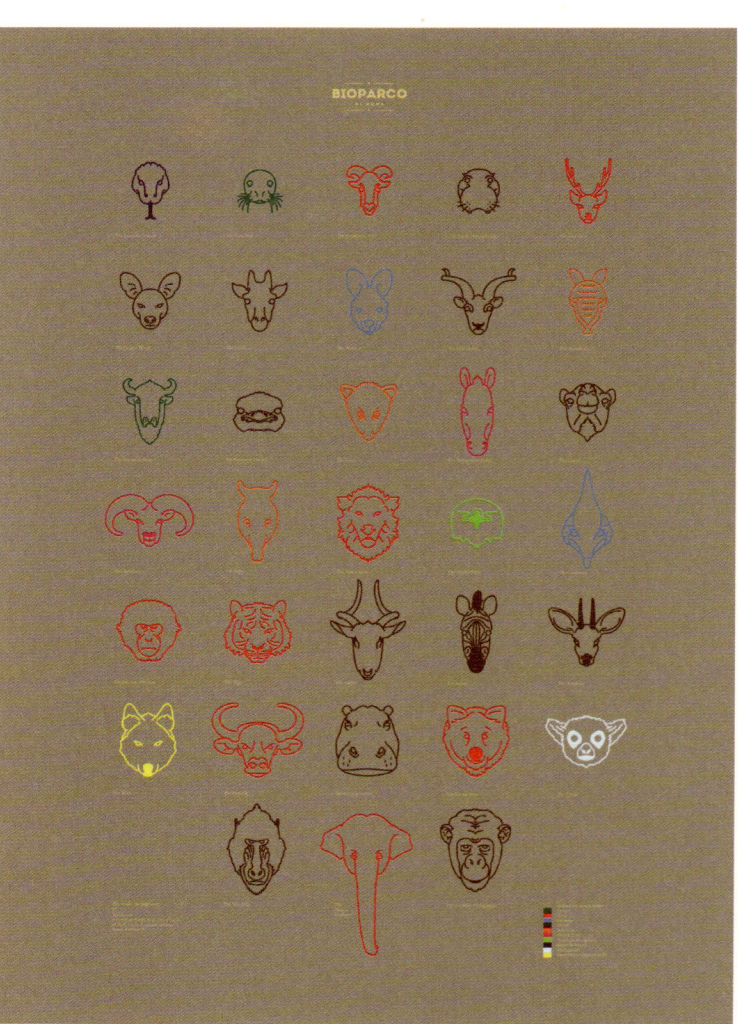

KOALA

Above (or below, depending on the relative placement of the picture) is the visual identity for a photographer who specializes in portraying Australian animals. This identity is inspired by the koala, an animal native to Australia. Designers merged a koala's face and the shape of a professional digital SLR camera in the logo to create an uncomplicated, yet playful feel.

STUDIO · UNKA

DESIGN · Vendula Klementova

MARÍA LEYVA FOTOGRAFÍA

This identity project puts on display the remarkable personality of the founder of the photo studio and her work, reflecting the powerful expression of her photographs and her love for nature. The logotype shows to be the letter "M" in a positive light and the synthesized image of a cat in a negative light, the letter representing the animal world.

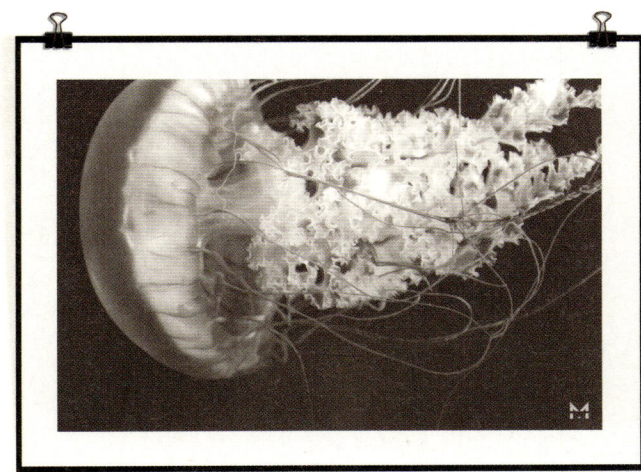

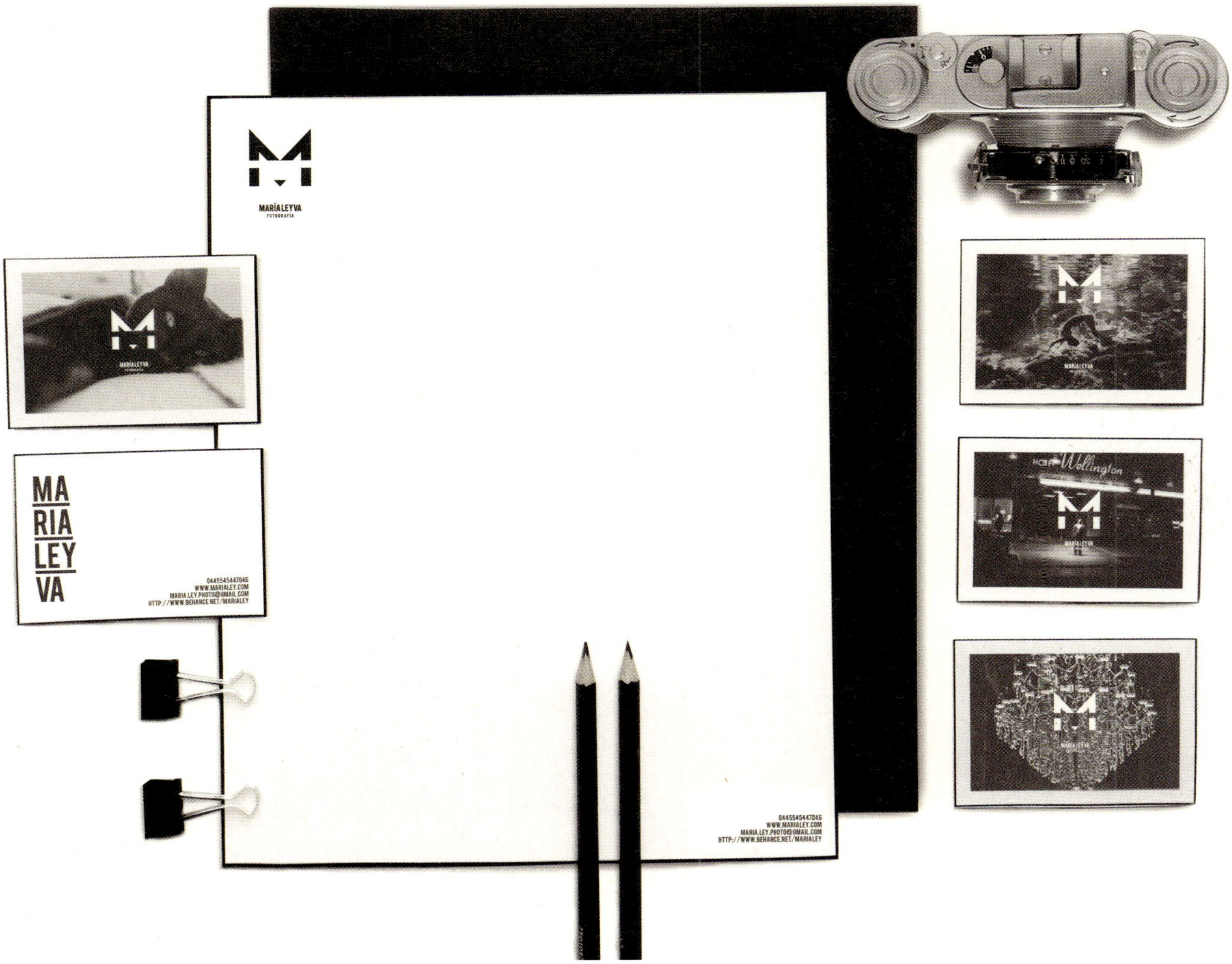

DESIGN · Karla Rocío. Heredia Martínez

THE DONKEY SANCTUARY

The Donkey Sanctuary is an international equine charity. Designers created an identity centered on donkeys and developed an illustration that communicates a feeling of safety, devotion and care.

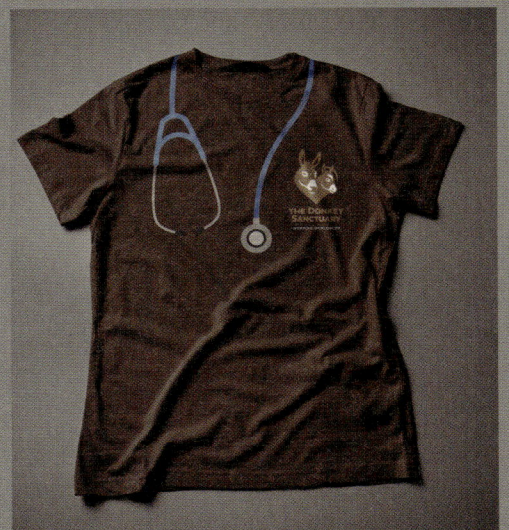

ANDALUZ

Andaluz is an audio/video production company which takes its name and identity from the surrealist movie Un Perro Andaluz ("An Andalusian Dog") by Luis Buñuel. For its logotype, a scratchboard, an A-shaped rocking horse is used to engender a monochrome image of non-linearity, noise and saturation.

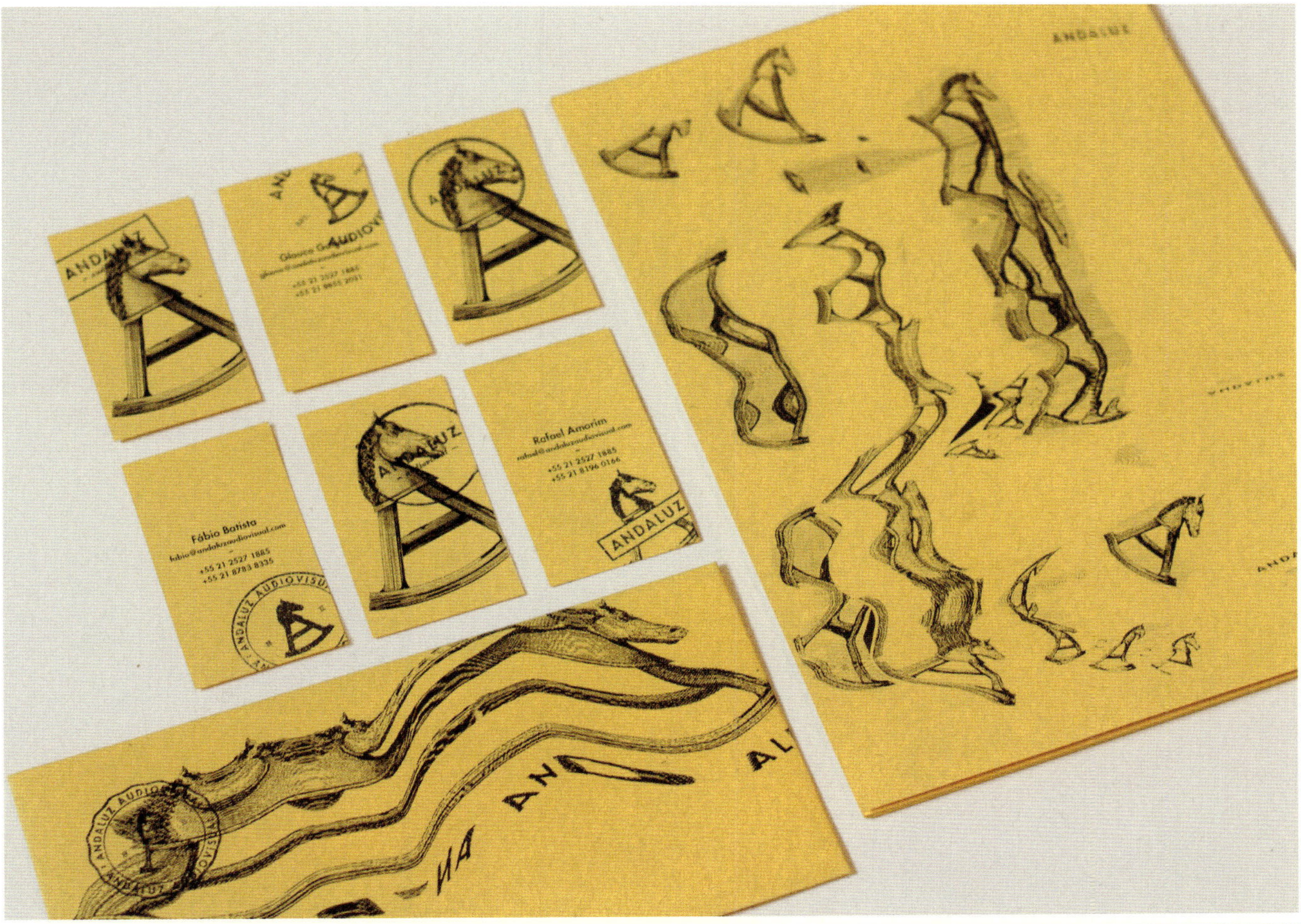

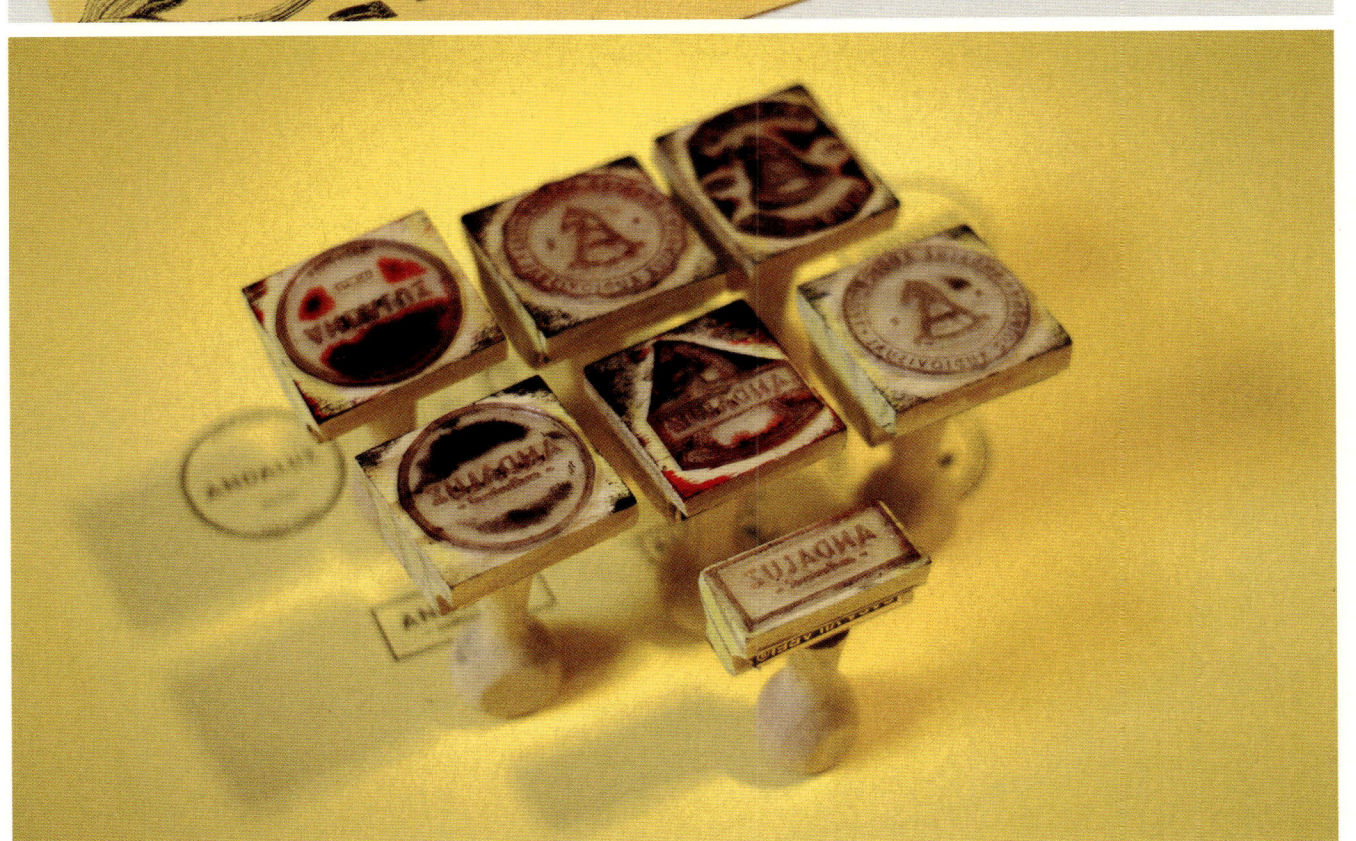

STUDIO · Plau

DESIGN · Eduardo Mattos, Luisa Borja, Rodrigo Saiani code: Caio Vaccaro, Gustavo Saiani, Luisa Borja

YOUNG LIONS ITALY 2013

The design is inspired by the mane that differentiates a young lion from a mature one. In nature, the mane grows larger and darker with age. The Young Lions competition represents an opportunity for talented designers to gain more experience, thus allowing their metaphorical mane to grow. Each one of the four colors represents a category of the competition.

DIGITAL   DESIGN   PRINT   FILM

WHITEBITES

Dog food package inspired by the designer's pet. The individuality of a dog is valued and blended into the package design. The combination of monochrome colors with vibrant hues is a vivid representation of the colorful life of having a pet at home.

DELIVERED BY HAND

"Delivered by Hand" is the first RSB-designed greeting card collection launched in 2013. The collection was inspired by alternative methods of visual communication, in which a single message or greeting can be conveyed. Using a vintage illustration of the ASL (American Sign Language), each of the ten gestures corresponds to a specific letter. These hand signals make the collection both aesthetically and intellectually interesting.

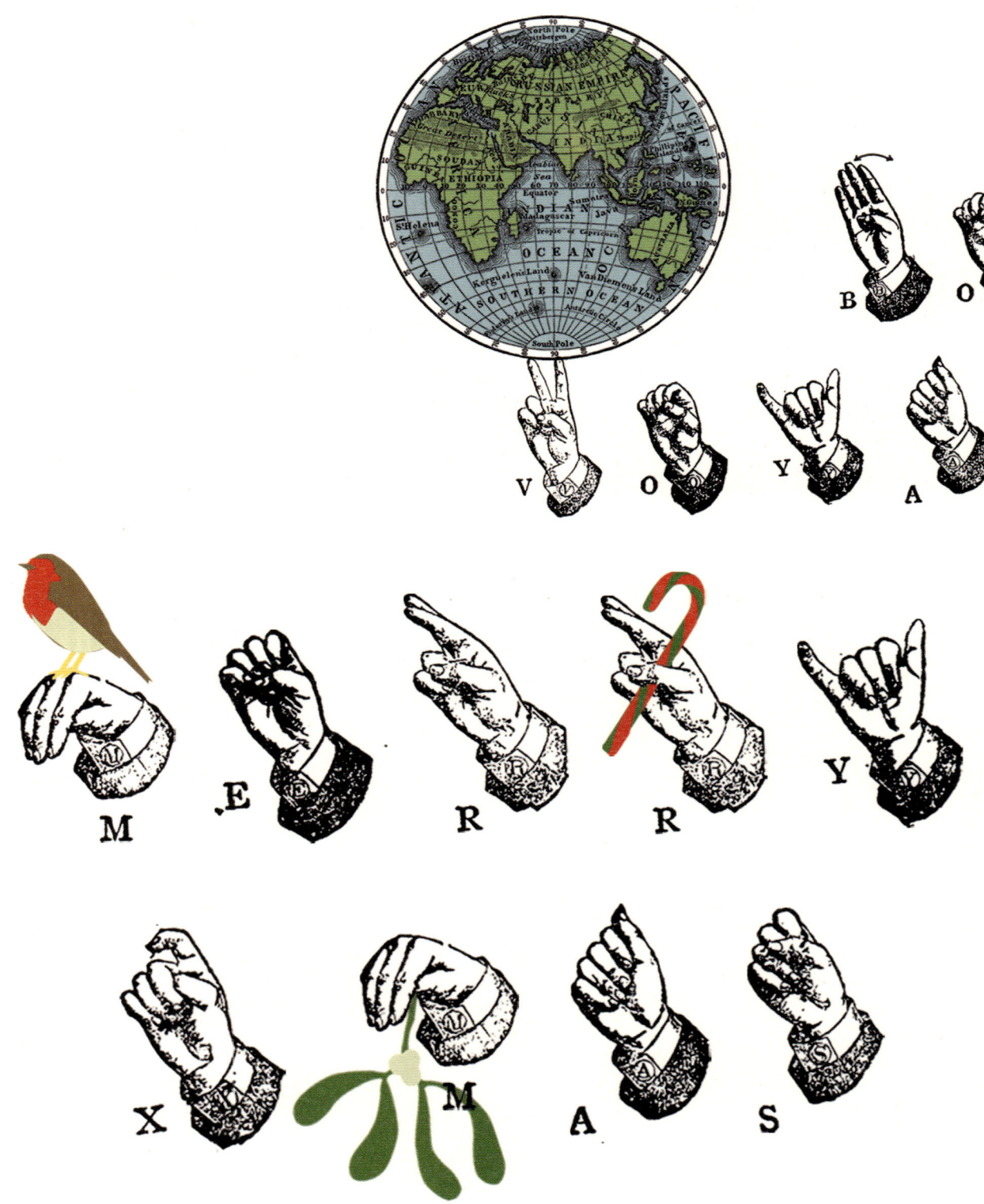

STUDIO · rsb designs

DESIGN · Ruth Scott-Beaulieu

LODZ DESIGN FESTIVAL 2012

Depicted is the visual identity for sixth Lodz Design Festival. The theme of the event was AWARENESS. It highlights the importance of the awareness in design, in addition to its usefulness and aesthetic value. To this end, designers chose chimpanzee as a representative who symbolizes the essence of reflection on reality and changes.

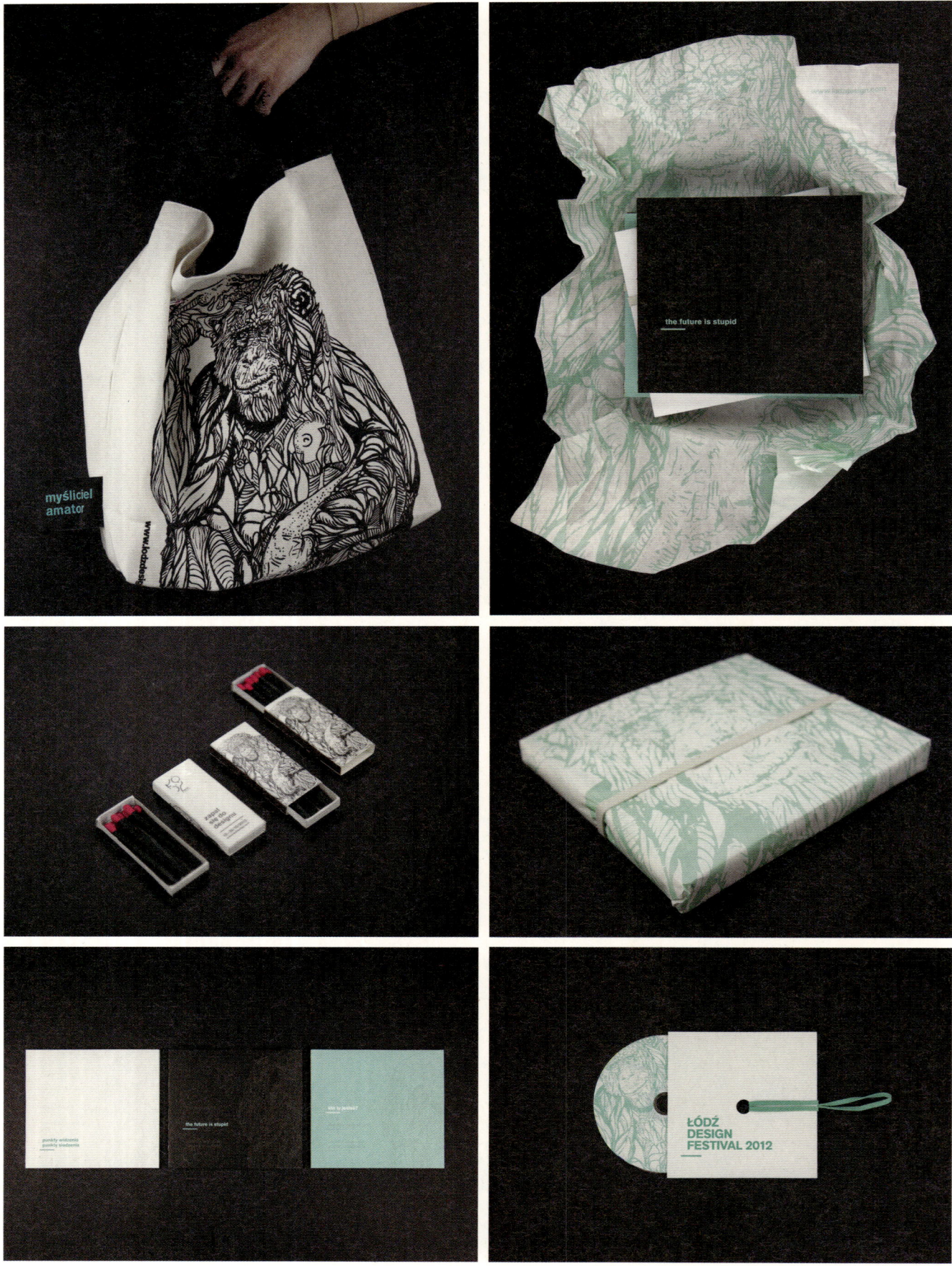

HORN OF PLENTY

Horn of Plenty is a visual identity for fashion designer Alexander McQueen's 2009 collection. The final design is based on the principles of surrealism, dada and postmodernism. Incompatible things are combined to obtain grotesque, unexpected results such as the scissor-fish. The goal was to break conventions, mixing classic beauty and natural beauty with the ugliness of technological progress.

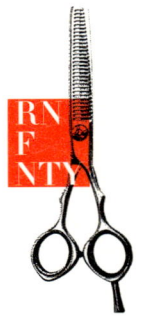

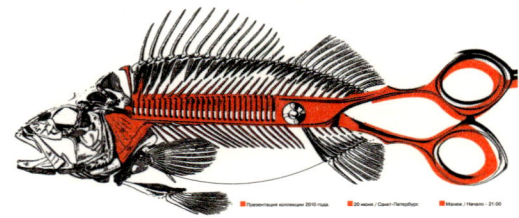

STUDIO · Saint-Petersburg state univercity

DESIGN · Artem Rulev

HAPPY GOATS FARM

Happy Goats Farm is a dairy brand that seeks to spread happiness through its products and promotional campaigns. A series of posters for it uses cheerful animal quotes to make the customer's smile. The pastel hues of this design create a relaxed, cozy atmosphere in which it is easier for customers to let down their guard and appreciate the joyful side of life.

LEGAJNY TOMATO FARM

Legajny Tomato Farm is a local Polish tomato producer. A classic and illustrative image of a tomato is applied in the symbol of the company to create a traditional look and a natural touch. The old-fashioned image of the brand is emphasized by the use of natural materials, such as felt, cotton, recycled paper, and cardboard.

LA GORDITA

La Gordita is a fine food distribution project inspired by Latin-American culture, their dynamic approach to street food, and delicious traditional meals. The goal was to create an identity that reflects the randomness of graphic patterns in the streets of Mexico. Reusing existing materials, such as old glass jars, the labels were made to adapt to any size and shape of supports, using paint and vinyl stickers.

DESIGN · Sarah Ouellet

VALENTTO

Valentto is Olivarera Italo-Mexicana's virgin olive oil brand destined for industrial kitchens and restaurant use. To counteract Valentto's tendency to lean overly much towards an industrial outlook, designers added beautiful Italian landscapes as the brand's background. The Italian country scenery not only serves to balance out the industrial coolness this brand would otherwise have, it also gives it natural warmth, an air of familiarity and tradition. The logotype fits snugly inside a diamond, giving it a tight, symmetrical feeling. Hot-pressed gold foil and uncoated, unbleached paper speak for the brand's high quality, cold-pressed, all natural extra virgin olive oil.

SKY CLUB

Corporate identity built on cloud-based imagery unifies fitness club Sky Club's communications, reflects and popularizes the club's vision of helping people to achieve physical and emotional harmony.

MONSTER CHOCOLATE CO.

Monster Chocolate Co. is a line of novelty chocolate products that are typically found in curiosity shops and specialty food stores. The designer wanted to explore what people consider to be real-life monsters and find the fascination, mystery and beauty within them. Customers are eventually convinced that these people are not monsters at all as they are portrayed in a way that demonstrates their beauty. Repeated Victorian hand-drawn patterns on gold packaging paper give this chocolate a truly decadent flare.

  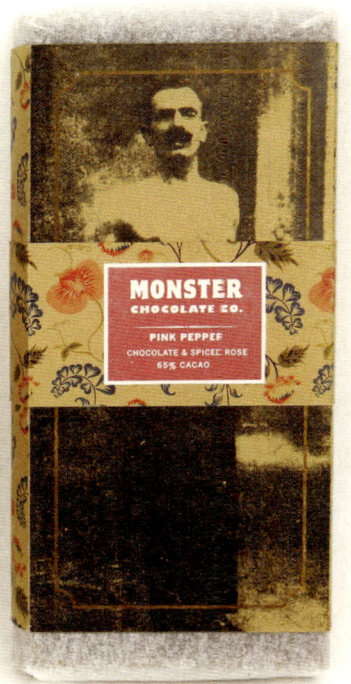
  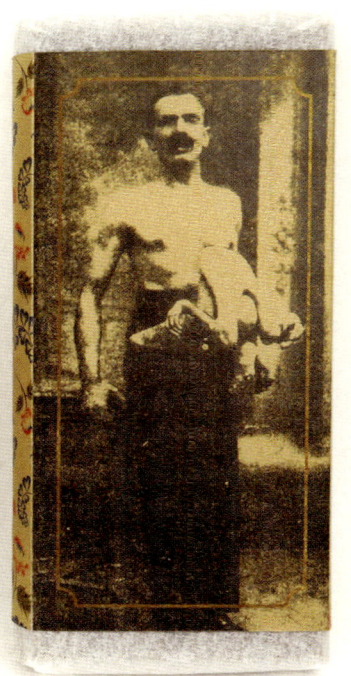

VIA SAUVAGIA

Via Sauvagia real estate is a mountainside residential district with a contemporary architectural style. The use of black and white biological elements, such as stones, wood, and plants embodies the eco-friendly concept of the brand.

DESIGN · Caroline Blanchette

AVALANCHE PRINT

Avalanche Print is an online platform that offers silk-printed tote bags and notebooks, with seven models and five colors to choose from. The design highlights the process of handmade silk printing and endeavors to popularize the technique again. Since the project is created around silk print, the choice of colors is very important. To go with the wintery appearance of the logo, blue has been chosen as the main color, becoming the heart of the project, not only applied on the products that they print, but also on all the media surrounding it (webiste, paper goods, etc.).

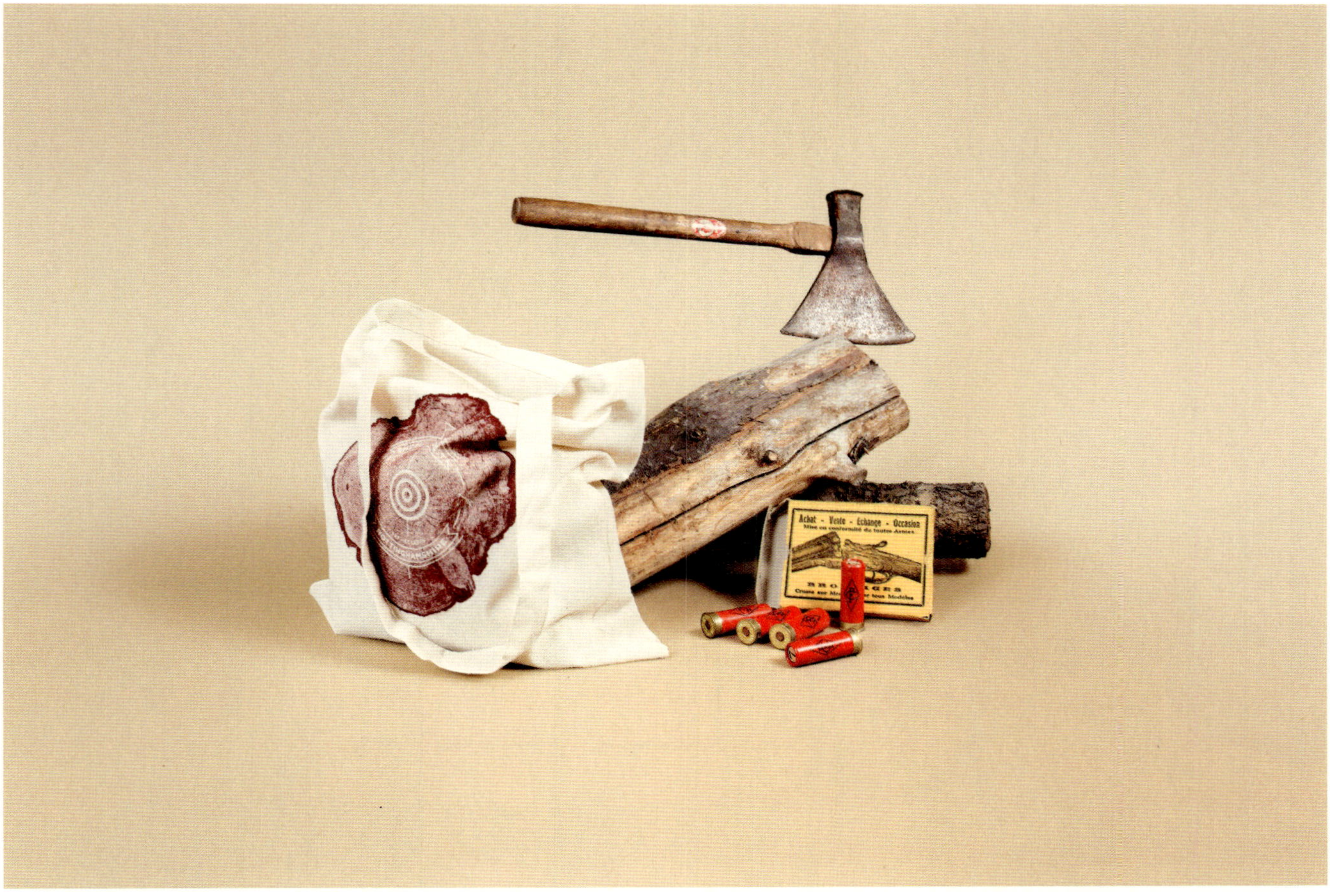

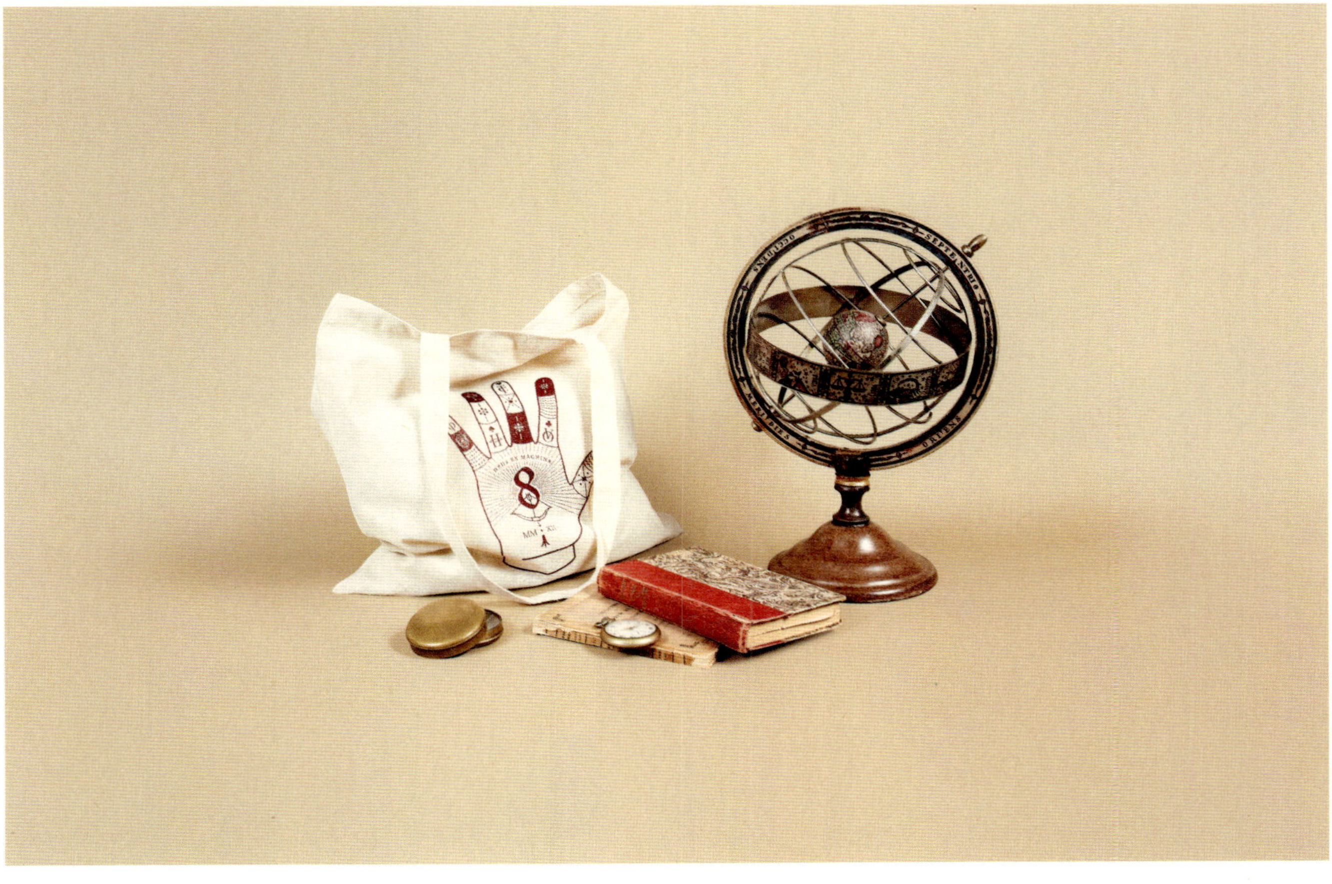

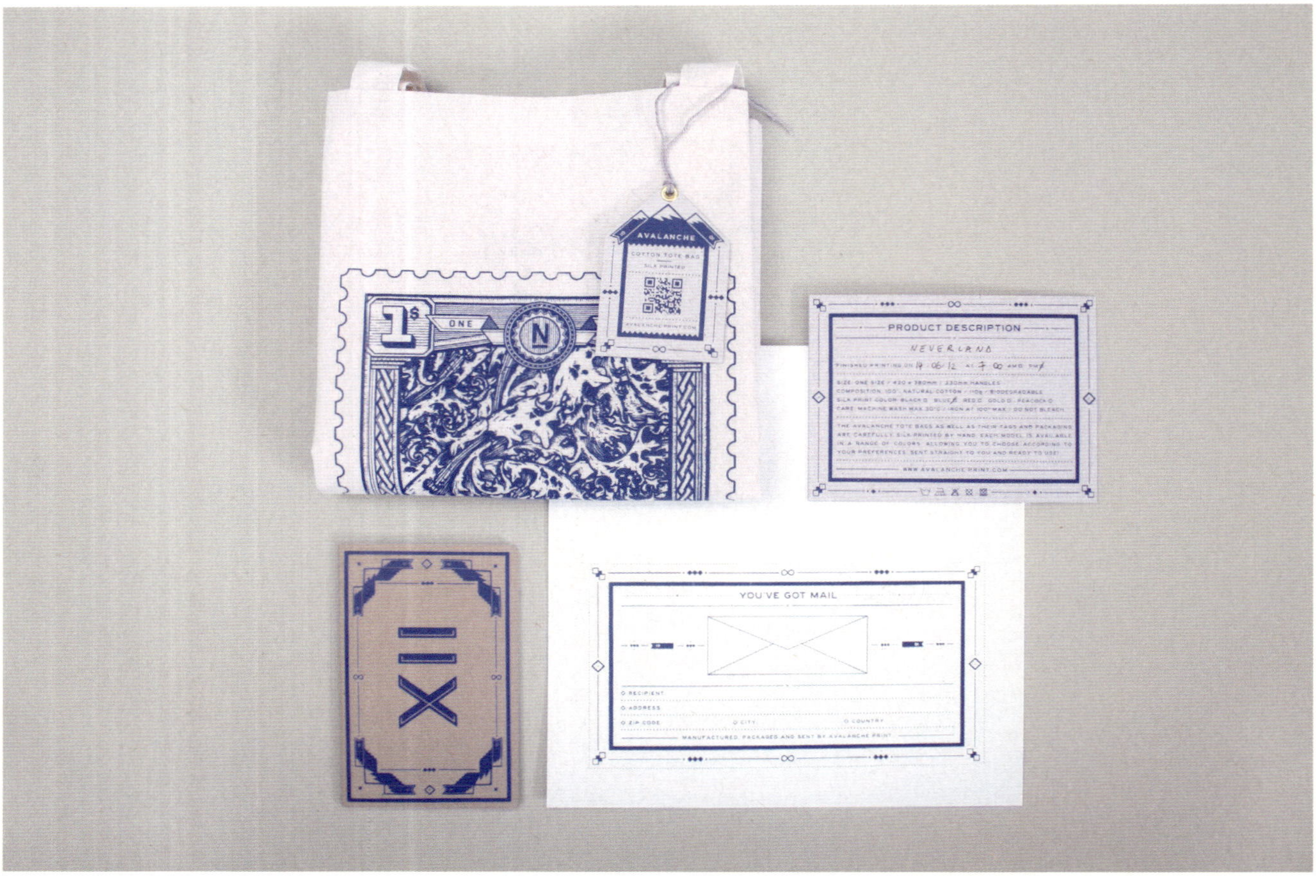

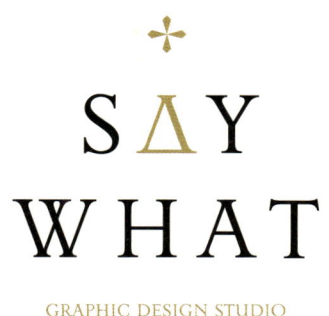

HAWTHORNE & WREN

Hawthorne & Wren specializes in producing meaningful gifts of consolation. A hawthorn symbolizes honor, respect, hope and the healing of broken hearts, since it is known for longevity and strength. The wren conveys a message of hope to those who grieve - thus the two elements are effectively used in the brand identity. The color scheme bolsters the handmade quality with its vitality.

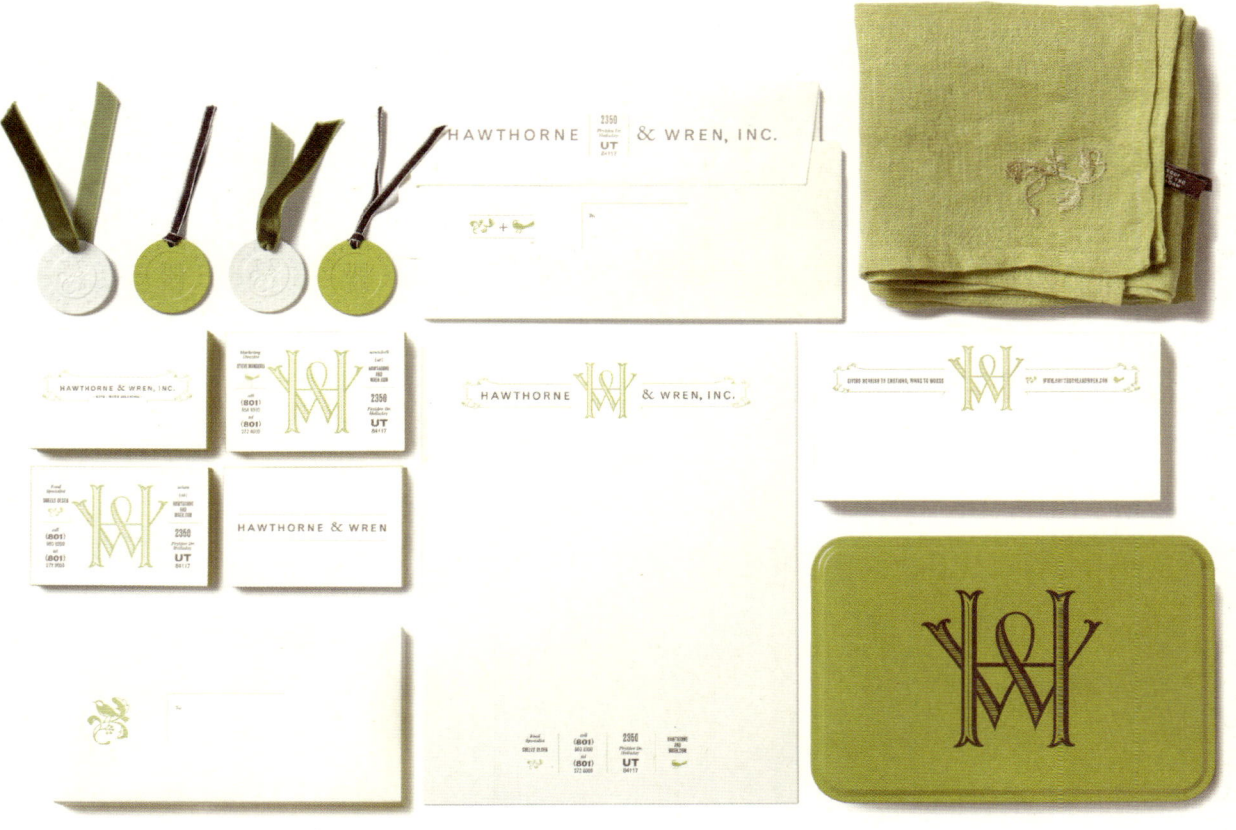

STUDIO · A3 Design
DESIGN · Kevin Cantrell

XXII BLACKENED WOOD

XXII Blackened Wood" is only one of a series of ugly, grungy fonts that were inspired by roots and branches and organic stuff.

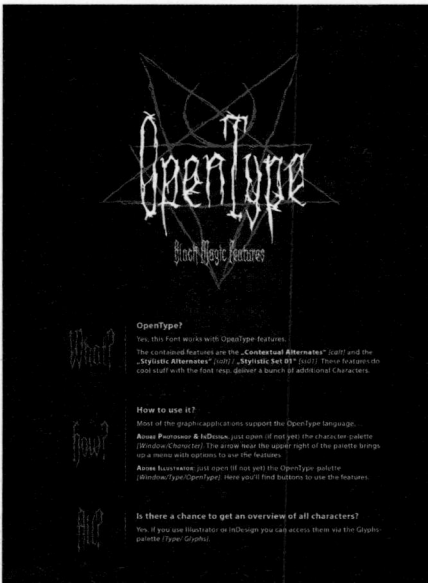

MARIA PIMENTA

Maria Pimenta is a typical Brazilian restaurant, named in memory of the owner's grandma. She used to cook very well by using a blend of flavors which often included peppers. The logo consequently consists of a pepper and the brand name in 3D relief.

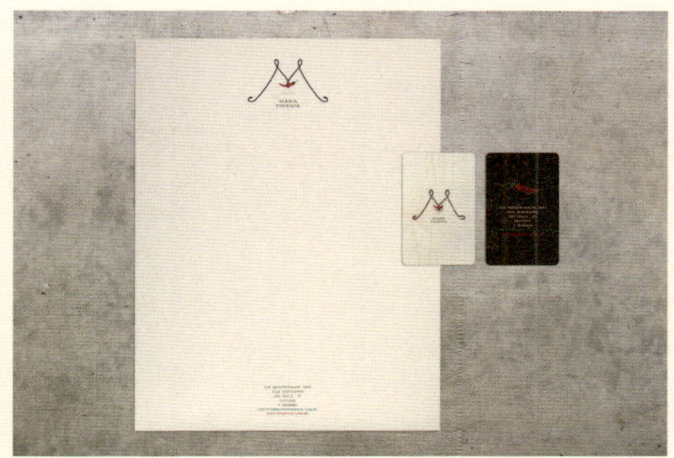

STUDIO · P/P Studio

DESIGN · Pedro Paulino

LACUE

The design for vegetable company Lacue located in Nagano, Japan is based on a head lettuce and map symbols, presenting a refreshing brand image.

GARDENHADA

Gardening has been perceived as an old-fashioned and not entirely appealing activity for the younger generation. Through the "gardenhada" project, designers tried to redefine gardening with images drawn in black ink lines, instead of using the actual photos of ripe fruits, to enhance the appeal to young people.

GARDEN IN THE HEAVEN

Garden in the Heaven ("Xianren zai" in Mandarin) is a sort of tea which caters to the tastes of high-end consumers. To respond to the mysterious and idyllic feel the brand conveys, the designer incorporated the image of a tea leaf into the logo with the use of Chinese landscape painting skills.

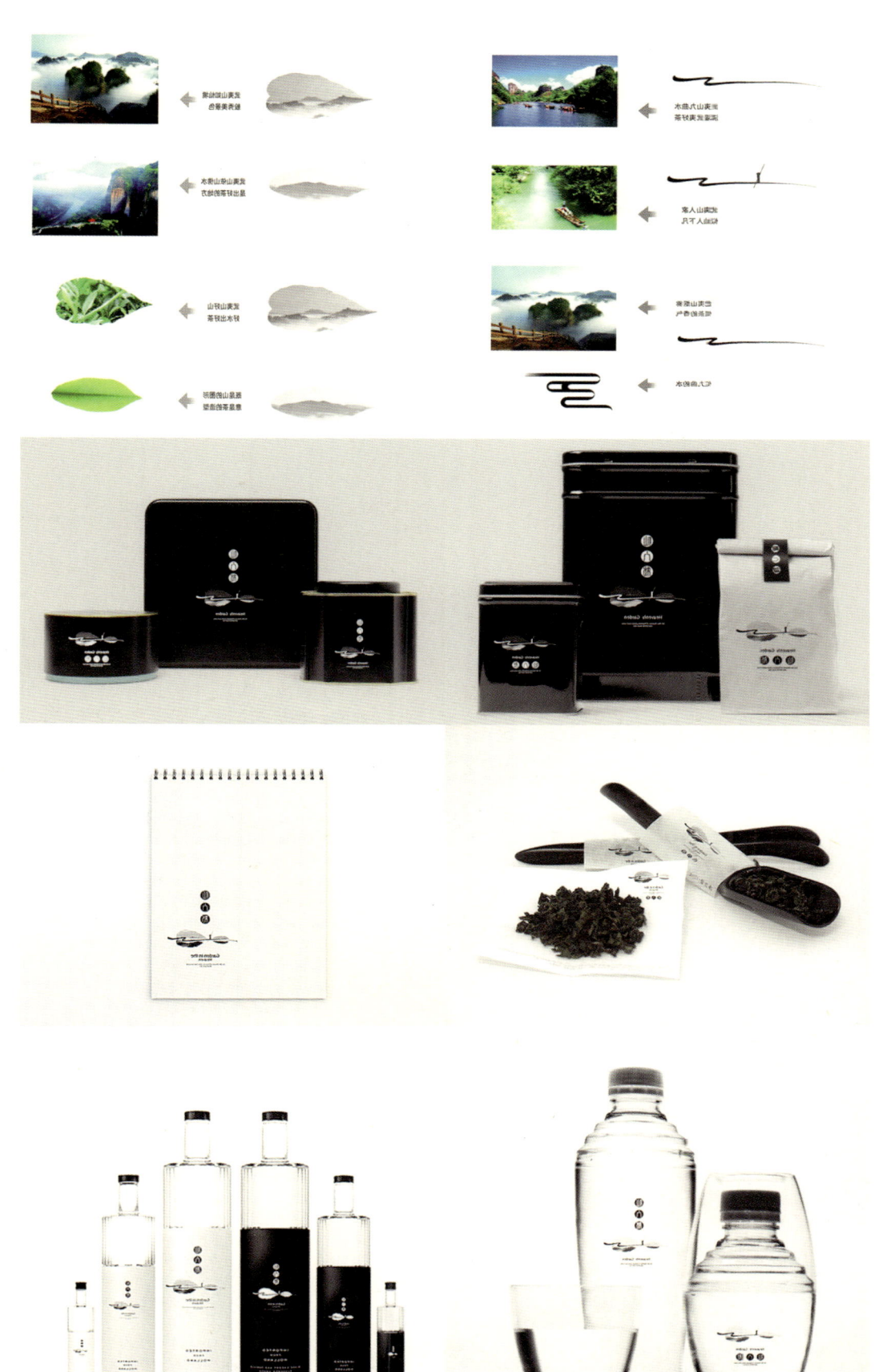

EXTREME SLOVENIA

Extreme Slovenia provides accommodation and organizes activities for extreme sports enthusiasts. Distinctively textured mountain-shaped patterns and an image resembling the sun are grouped in ES's brand identity, showing admiration for nature.

STUDIO · Supafrank

DESIGN · Vicki Turner, Katie Steel

UNCUT PICTURES

Branding and identity for film-editing studio Uncut Pictures, the design was inspired by the dramatic footage of a magnificent mountain.

UNCUT/PICTURES

SOY MAMELLE

Soy mamelle is a 100% vegetative product. The shape of the package resembles an udder, presenting the natural attribute of the product. The green cow markings employed on the packaging create the impression of nature and health.

STUDIO · KIAN brand agency

DESIGN · Konstantinov Kirir

BEELOVED HONEY

Packaging for Beeloved Honey is simple, clean and effective. Its inspiration derives from natural world, to be specific, a piece of rock, raw gemstone, diamond and honeycomb.

DESIGN · Tamara Mihajlovic

NATURE GRAPHICS

Micro World

Sight is limited, but the search for beauty is a never-ending exploration.

In the world we inhabit, most creatures and objects - stone, dirt, trees, raindrops, and plants - are distinguished as pretty, plain or ugly. Most people are content with such cognizance and are therefore ignorant of a world filled with curiosity and wonders beneath the seeming mediocrity.

Without a microscope, human eyes can only see things bigger than a tenth of a millimeter. Anything smaller than that will elude our sight and comprehension. The creatures and phenomena not directly detectable by human senses are referred to as "micro-creatures" and "micro phenomenon", constituting the micro domain.

On the one hand, the fascinating view science has opened our eyes to -- the colors, intricate structures, components, permutations and combinations hidden from our sight, has not only expanded our knowledge of the world, but also reinvented our understanding of beauty,. For every discovery is one-of-a-kind, enticing people to study, inspiring scientists, artists, and designers to create, and ultimately leading change and greater imagination in civilization.

On the other hand, new recording facilities enables close examination which is not restricted by the limits of human perception, facilitating the observation and discovery of minute shapes, textures, varying colors and details that will create a brand new visual experience for the public, extending and challenging the visual presentation of the traditional aesthetic standards.

Public attention is nowadays the shortcut to profit. Apart from fulfilling design requirements, designers - graphic designers in particular - are required to attend to the visual and psychological appeal of the work. The masses are weary of overwhelming information, be it textual or visual, actively or passively received, and are therefore reluctant to invest

time or energy on it. A new, refreshing approach to restoring the public's image is to open their eyes to the curiosities which exist in the micro world, as well as continuing the study of visual and cultural perceptions.

There is a micro-world on this planet that twinkles with the wisdom of reason and shines with the beauty of sensitivity, and to us, it is a mysterious and awe-inducing source of inspiration to explore for the purpose of change and innovation.

MAKLERSOZIETÄT WORM UND PARTNER

MAKLERSOZIETÄT Worm und Partner focuses on providing personal insurance. Tree bark depicted in this company's signage hints at the tough conditions of the insurance industry. Connecting lines visualize brokers' daily work - professional comparisons between complex insurance products.

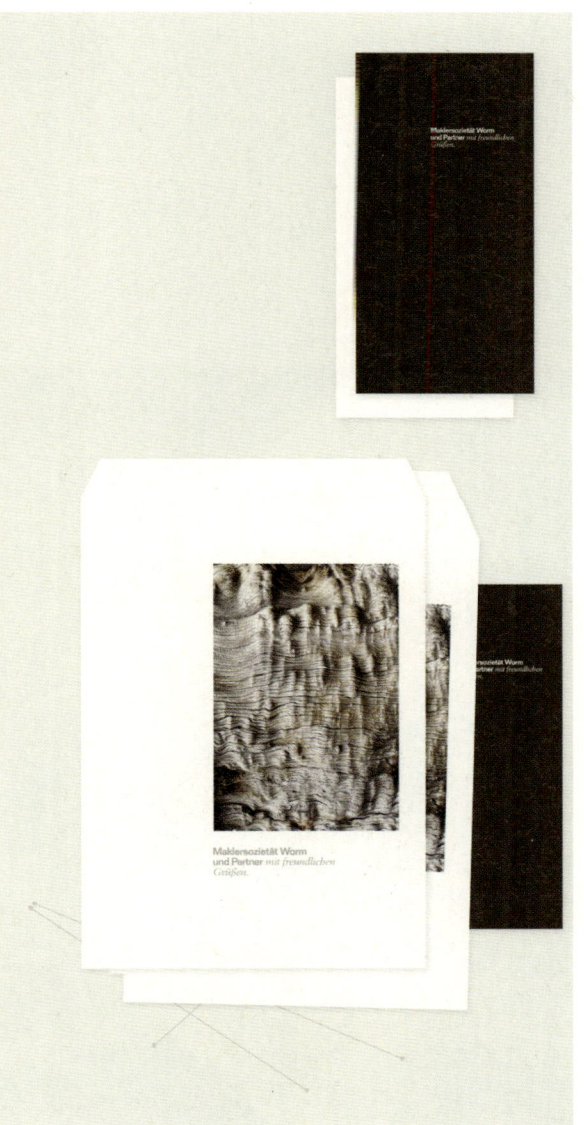

NOVELTY

Novelty is a boutique that retails casual wear for chic young women. Watercolor marks and black & white collages mark its brand identity. Through these elements the shop reveals its elegantly sophisticated taste.

GRAZIA

Grazia is an eatery in Bogotá, Colombia where food lovers can buy refined sweets and savory delicacies. The challenge of this project was to create a visual language that honors the beauty and perfection of the fare. Designers visited the local market with the chefs, picked out vegetables and fruits, and went to the chef's house to cut and photograph the food. The second element of the design is lines, which show the spatial structure of the objects and provide a point of reference for the logo.

STUDIO · P576
DESIGN · Arutza Rico, María Silva

PACT

PACT is a co-branded venture and partnership between like-minded businesses located in Singapore's Orchard Central shopping center. The marble texture was chosen to depict its hairstyling, food and fashion businesses converging into a united whole. The swirls and mixes within the marble highlight the brand's spontaneous yet unwavering vision of partnerships.

MUTUO

Mutuo is the collective of two architects. Their work is characterized by experimental solutions in the diverse fields of architecture and design. The dynamic identity design reflects their new architectural experiences through chaos and the blend of their different roots with the use of flowing fluid and an organic combination of rather dissimilar objects.

ESKIMO

Eskimo is a Russian design studio. Since in Russian "ЭСКИМО" (Eskimo) means "choc-ice" (chocolate ice cream), the main color scheme of the identity consists of maroon, black and brown. The sleek wood boxes inspire viewers to get out into the world of nature.

ECOPRODUCTS TO GALLECS

Package design for ecological agriculture products by Gallecs Association. Aiming to reduce environmental impact and cost, efforts have been made to facilitate and separation of the waste. The paper are mostly recycled and chlorine-free, following environmental criteria, using a single ink and incorporating different recipes on the back of the label, maximizing its usage.

NÚRIAVILA . ESPAI CREATIU

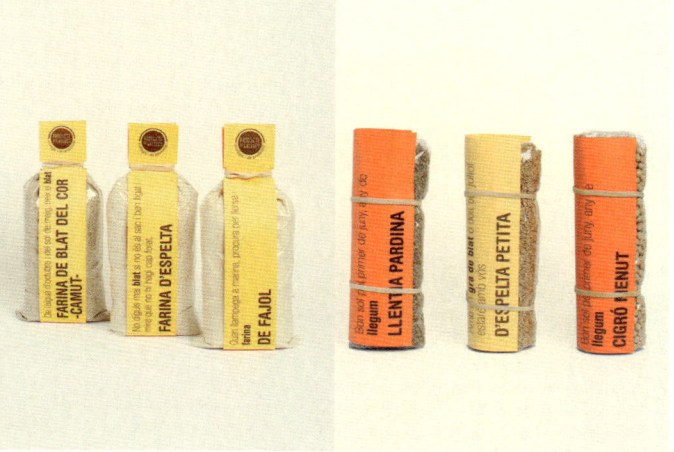

DESIGN · Núria Vila, Laura Rodriguez

EVA SOLO – FOOD MEETS FUNCTION

In 2012, Eva Solo launched a series of kitchenware that met the qualifications of professional chefs as well as its uncompromising design standards. The designers used the cooking utensils and food as focal elements to create a remarkable visual effect through reconfiguration. Food meets function in this gastronomical realm.

Packaging / Eva Solo XO Collection 03

FOOD MEETS FUNCTION

STUDIO · Bessermachen DesignStudio

DESIGN · Kristin Brandt

VÅRDAPOTEKET

Vårdapoteket is a Swedish pharmacy chain. To distinguish themselves from the depressing environment common to hospitals, SDL developed a soft new identity inspired by the human body. Organ patterns in bright shades are widely used in the wallpaper, packaging and other decorations.

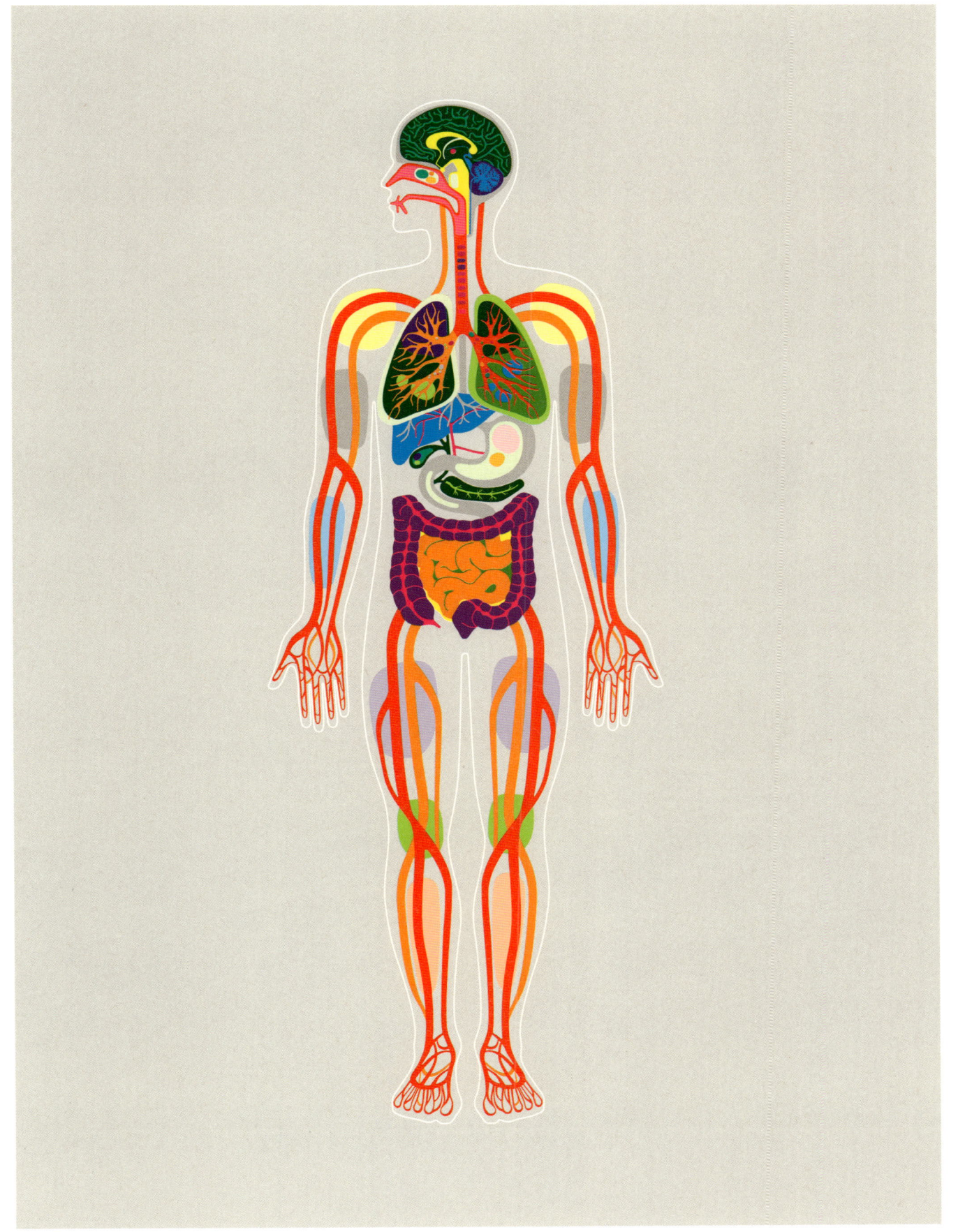

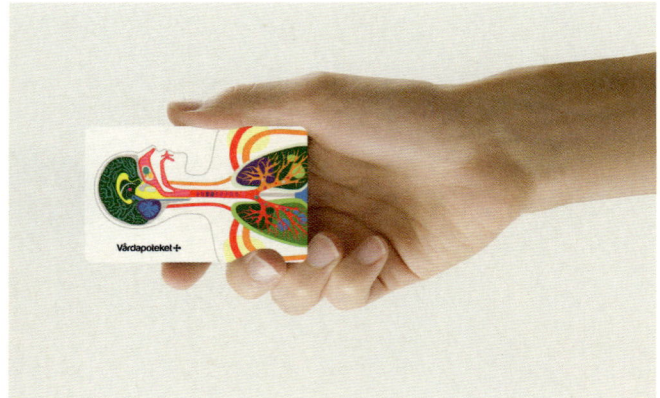
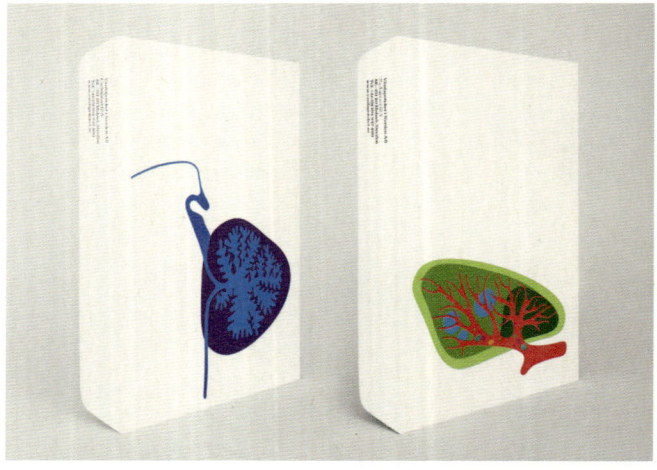

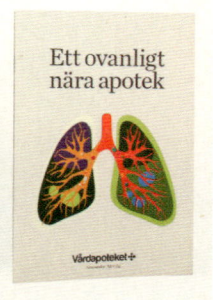

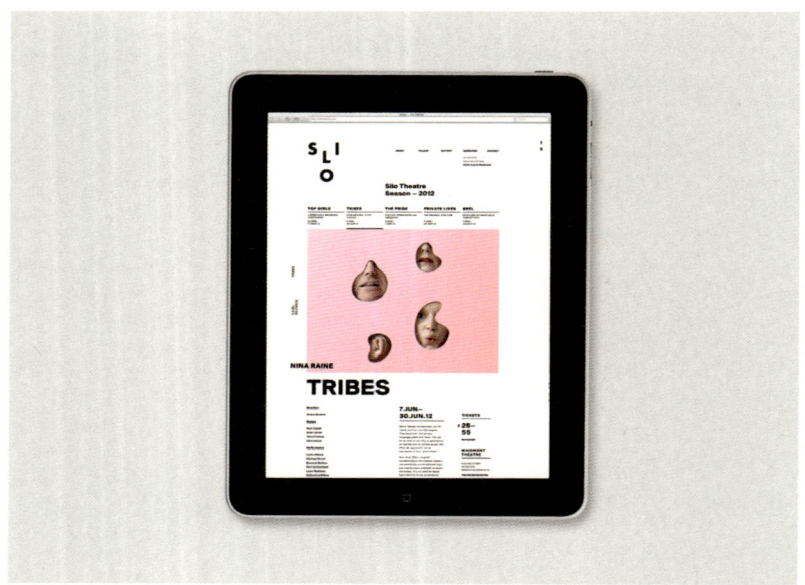

SILO THEATRE

The Silo logo has been composed by arranging the letters of its name to depict an image of a face. The "S" illustrates a wink, the "I" an eye, the "L" a nose and the "O" a mouth. Instead of the customary laughing or weeping face, this logo chooses facial expressions which emanate shock. This illustrates the theater's ambition of performing contemporary plays that will challenge the audience.

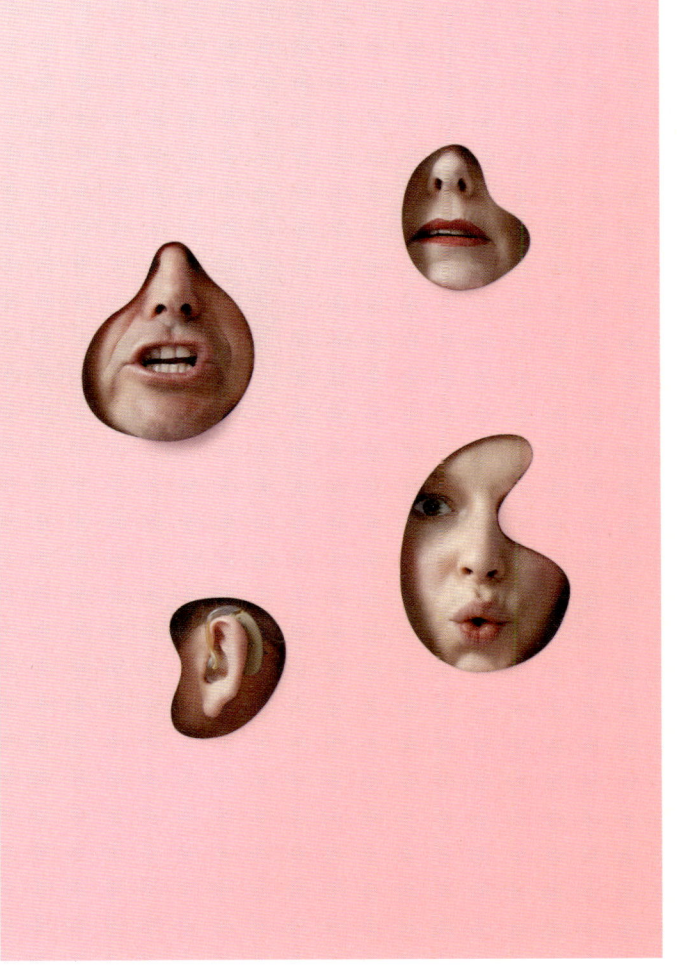

STUDIO · Alt Group

DESIGN · Dean Poole, Anna Myers, Emma Hickey, Aaron Edwards, Alan Wolfgramm, Kris Lane, Sons & Co.

LIQUID TYPE

In the typeface design, letters come to life: black lines flow around gray coral-like patterns and then disappear – like a caterpillar turning into a butterfly and then dying, or like a bizarre dance of life between birth and death. This font's beauty lies in its fluidity and evanescence.

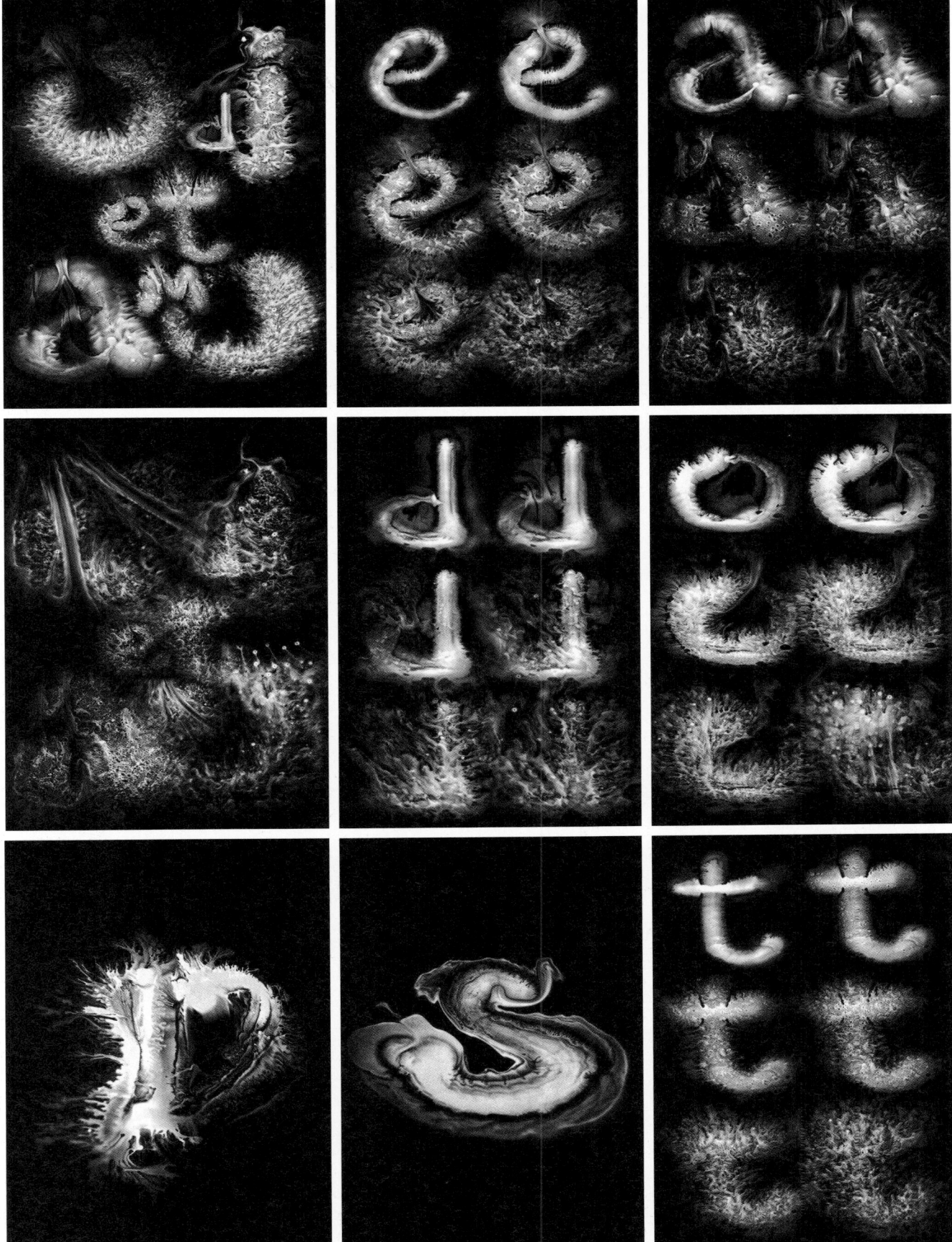

DESIGN · Ruslan Khasanov

SALVATIERRA

Salvatierra ("earth saver" in Spanish) specializes in producing quality organic goods. The logo is a pair of hands holding a mixture of snowflakes and plants, which is in allusion to nature protection. The packaging is inspired by soil, reflective of organic products.

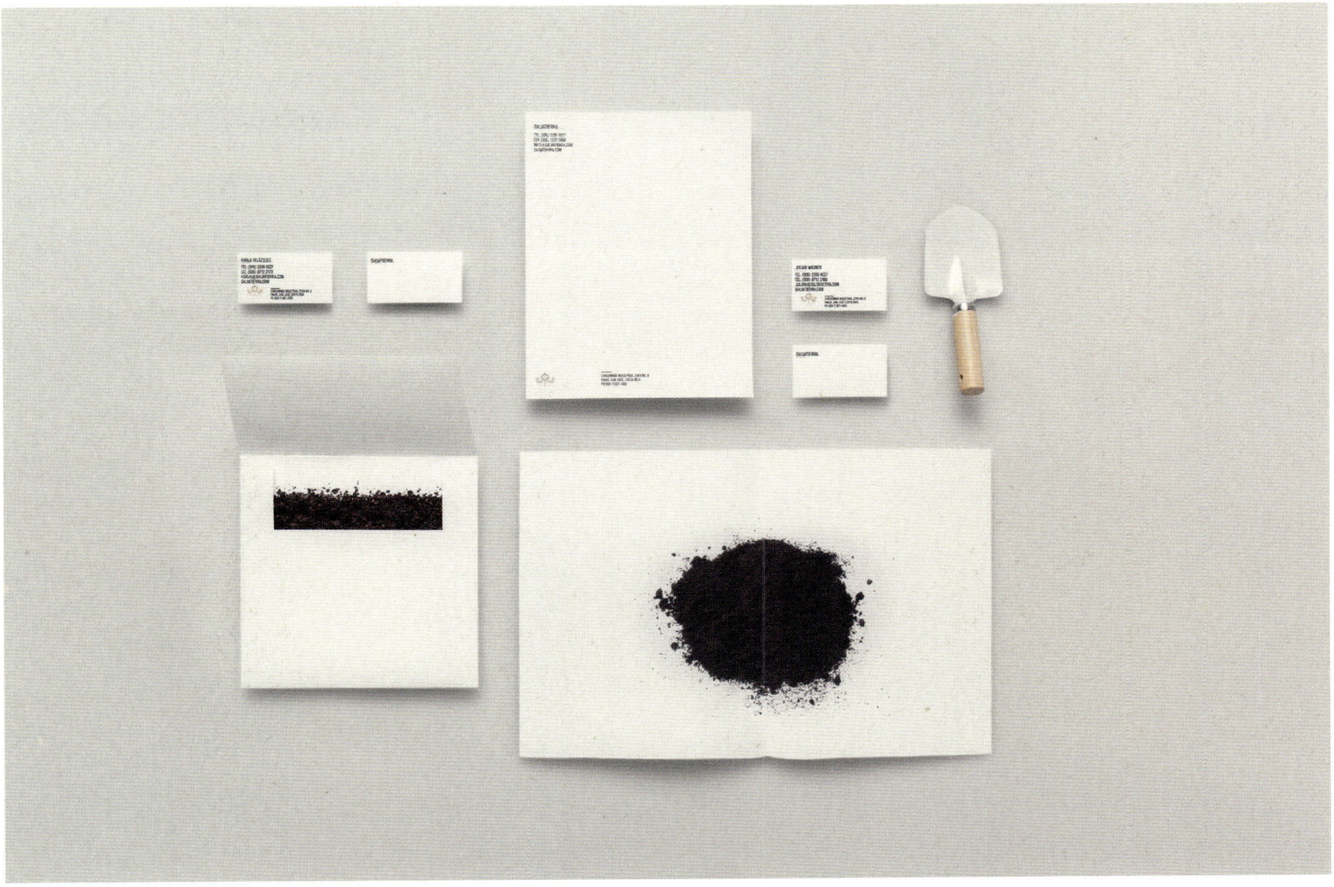

STUDIO · Anagrama

VISIT NORDKYN

Branding and identity for the promotion of Nordkyn, a tourist destination in Norway, contains the striking feature of a constantly updated weather statistic attached to the ice-cube-like logo. Similarly impressive is their slogan "where nature rules".

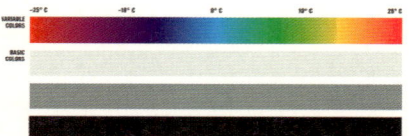

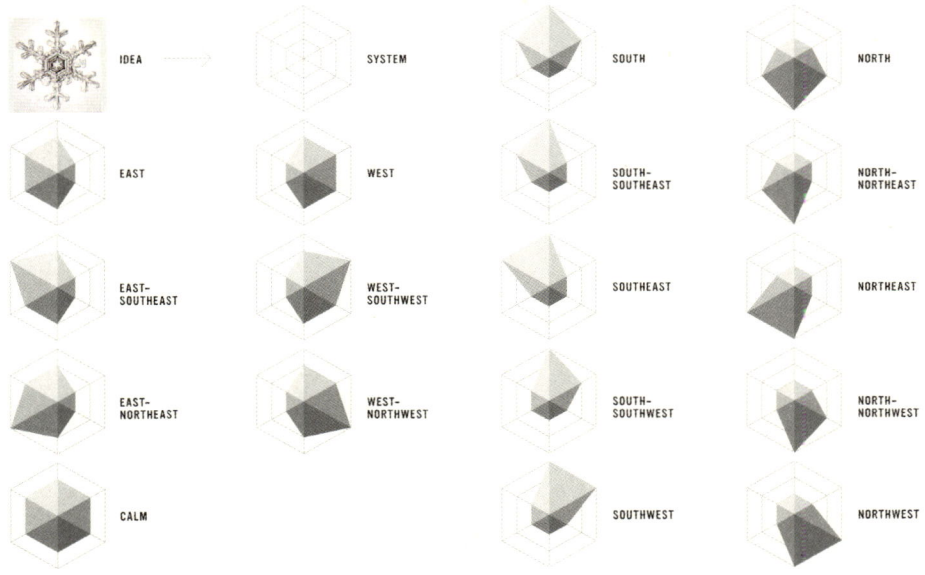

ULTRA-MAGNETIC

71°08'02"N

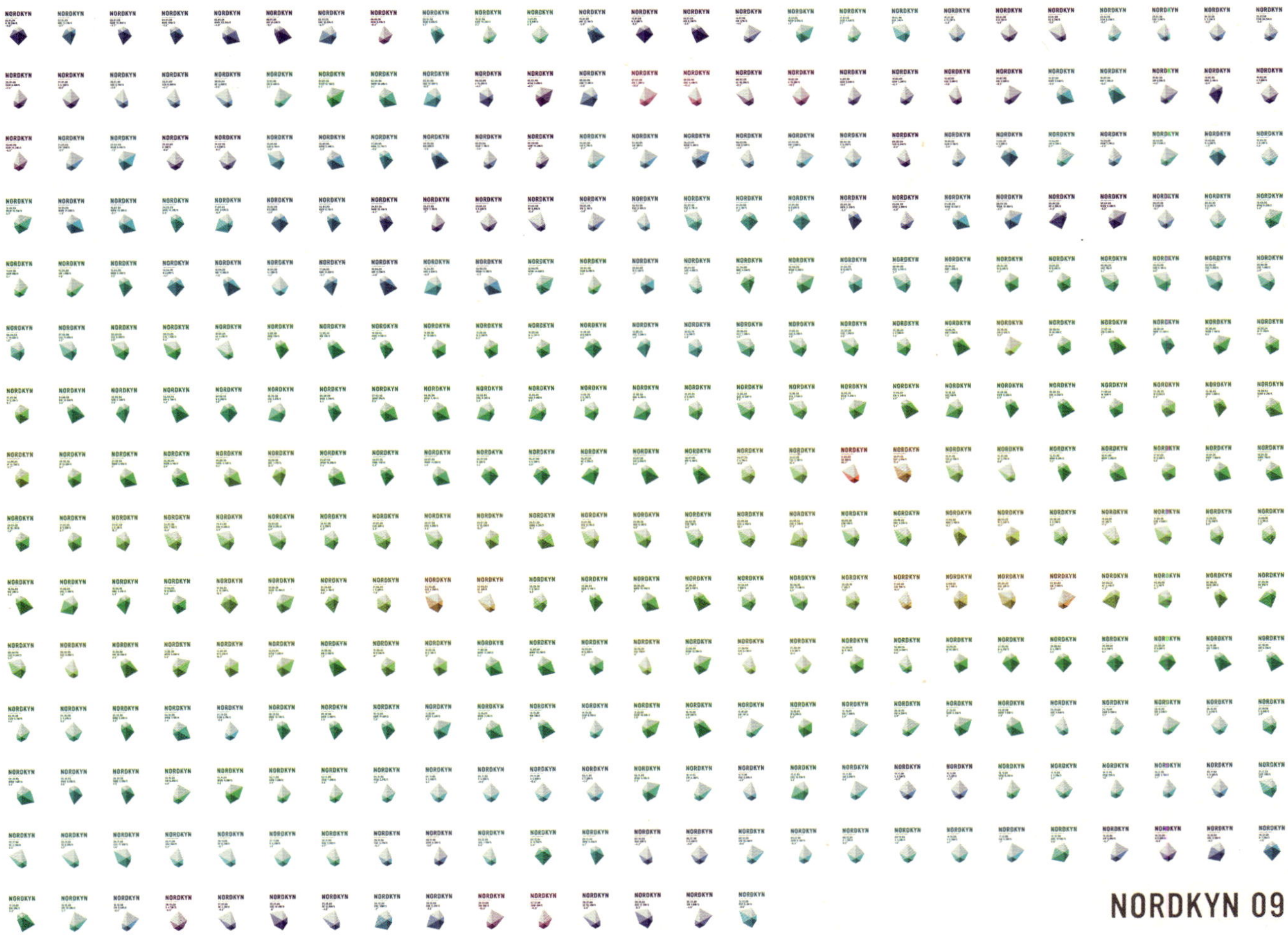

NORDKYN 09

THE GUARDIANS

Branding and identity for a new wine made by a prestigious winemaker family gained inspiration from an age-old vineyard guardian: the scarecrow. Different images of scarecrows were artistically created and bestowed a modern feeling through elements such as a grey suit, a golden gown and brown sackcloth.

BU YI

The clothing brand Bu Yi cherishes original natural beauty. This is reflected in its brand identity design through the bold use of microscopic leaf patterns. Those elements adequately infuse into the identity a sense of primitiveness and simplicity.

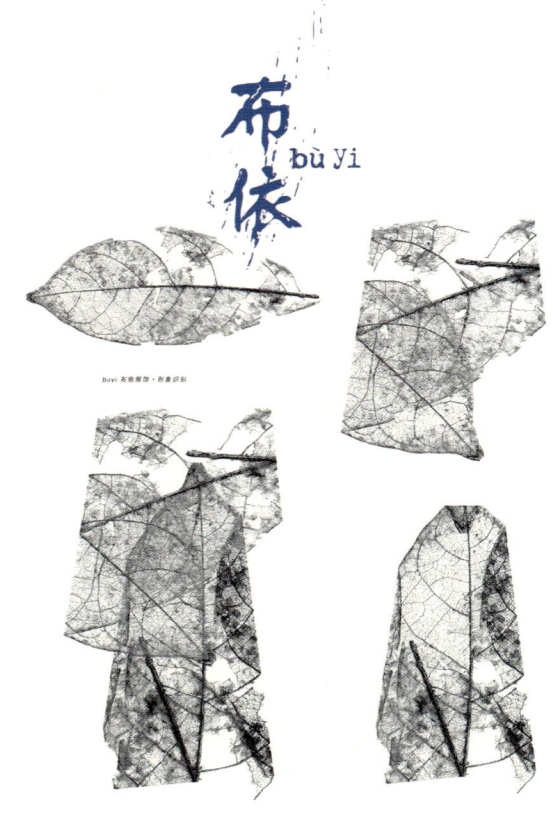

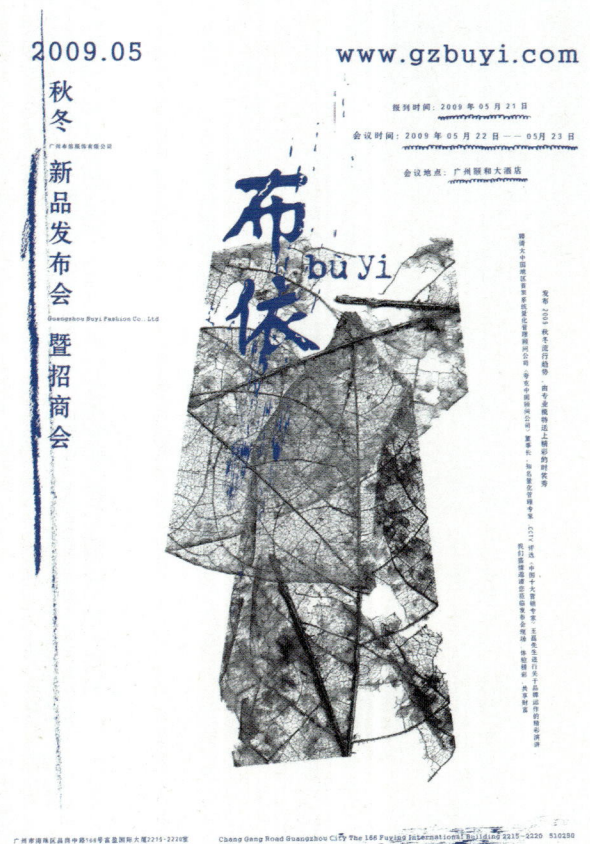

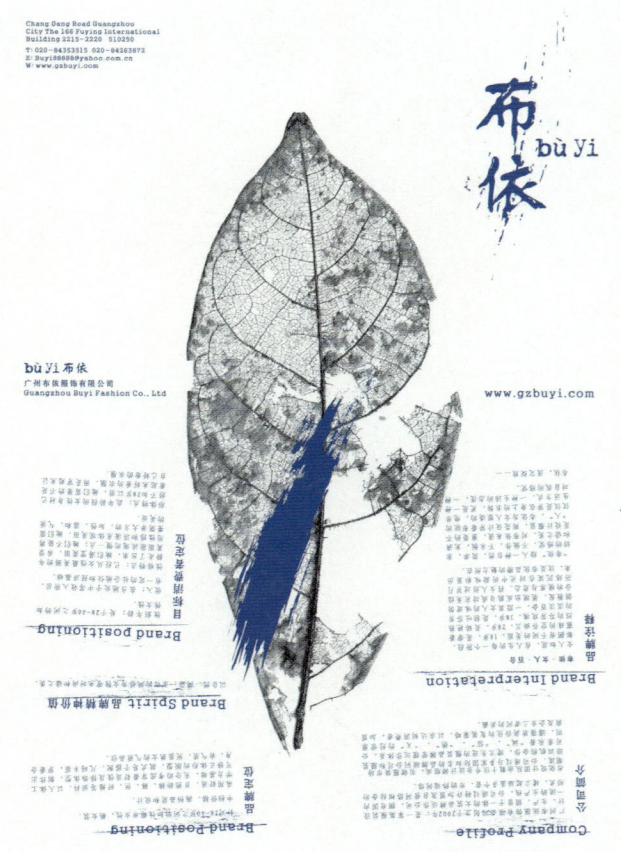

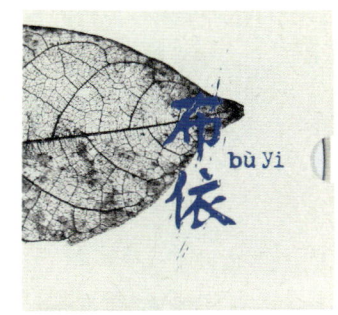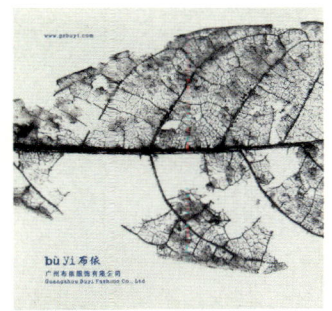
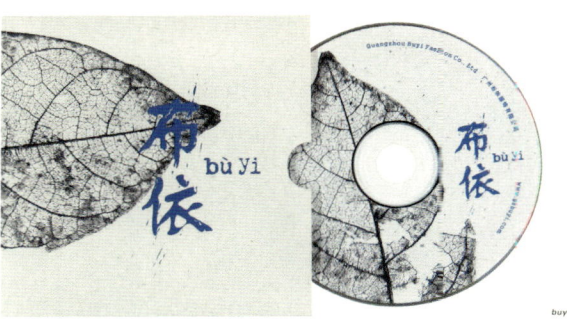

buyi 布依服饰·活动CD

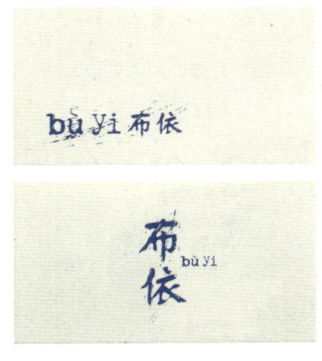

STUDIO · momonini creative space
DESIGN · Mao Zhigao, Li Tingting

HERBARIUM

Herbarium is a women's clothing shop which is well-known for its use of natural fabrics. Those fabric elements are mainly linen, cotton, wool and leather. Leaf-fiber patterns printed on the packaging, brochure and wallpaper reflect the respect for nature held by the shop.

TEXTURES COLLETTIVA CONTEMPORANEA

A visual identity was displayed for Textures Collettiva Contemporanea - a multicultural festival held in Airola (Benevento, Italy). Besides the exhibition of such contemporary art works as sculptures, paintings, video art and photography in this festival, there were meetings with writers, interviews, performances and live concerts. Stylists applied delicate natural textures to represent different art forms.

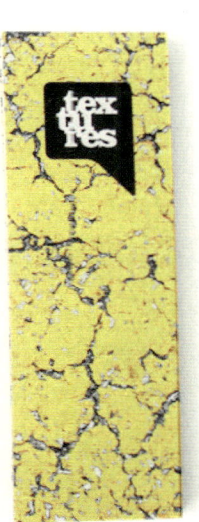

DESIGN · Giuseppe Fierro

OAT SHOES

OAT is the first biodegradable sneaker in the world. Once you wear them out, you can put them on the ground and they will not only decompose back to nature, but blcom because of the seeds embedded in them.

PRYSME

This self-designed brand identity aims to illustrate PRYSME's design philosophy. Designers at PRYSME dove into nature's depths to find ideas, which were then incorporated into the design.

ARTPHY

Artphy is a modern new art and philosophy center. As the starting point of the design, cobalt blue marks a selective range of vegetable's cross sections and symbolizes the void, infinity and absolute freedom.

STUDIO · BURO RENG
DESIGN · Hans Gerritsen, Pascal Rumph

MAYA SUNNY HONEY

Maya Sunny Honey is a 100% raw honey brand. The packaging design needs to be a full demonstration of the sustainable handcrafted process of the production of the beehive, jar and the honey itself. A locally obtained vine wire was selected to seal the neck of each jar as well as 100% recycled environment-care matte labels from KWDoggetts.

Maya Sunny
HONEY

100% raw

STUDIO · Zé Studio

DESIGN · Joe Tarzia

VITA MEDIC

Vita Medic is a medical clinic that provides specialized anti-aging medical care. The logo and corporate identity develcp around a lotus flower, which represents the rebirth of beauty.

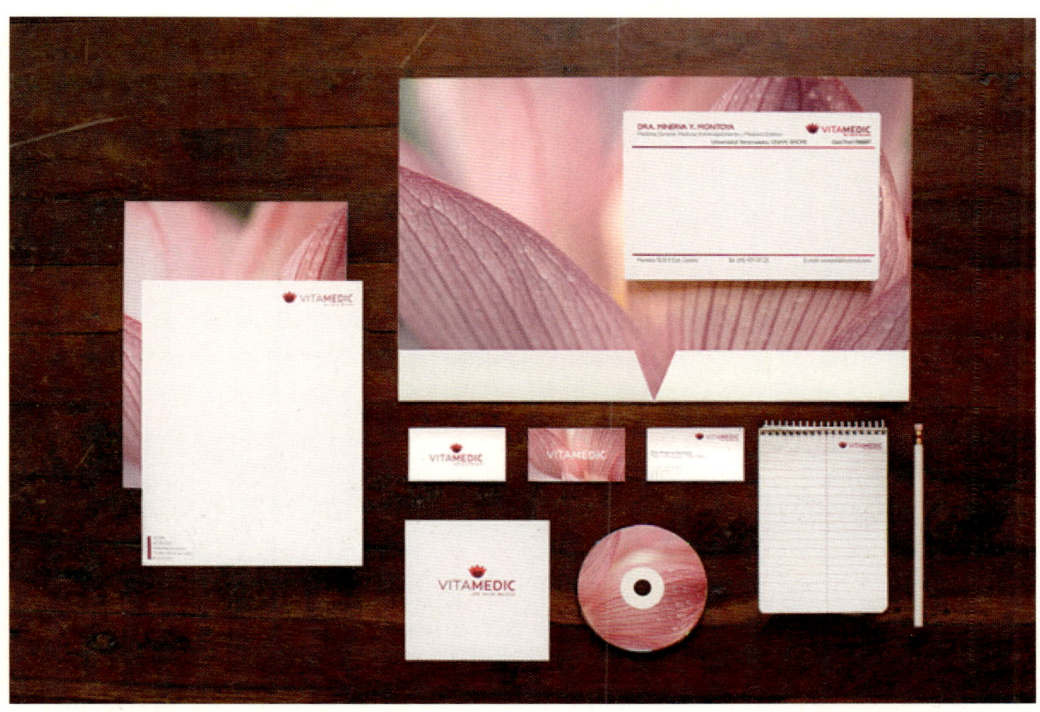

DESIGN · Elisa Ortiz

VI NOVELL 2012

Traditionally in Spain, in November, coinciding with the celebration of the pig slaughtering, the Vi Novell is bottled. It is a fresh and fruity wine bottled before its fermentation process is complete. To respond to the background, a raw meat fiber pattern was used in the packaging and poster.

MEAT CHARTS

This is a series of new meat charts designed for the Swedish meat brand "Svenskt Kött". In order to more closely resemble actual dishes on the table rather than simply displaying objective information on the wall, designers used dissected pig, beef and lamb as the main elements of the charts.

Nöt
(Lat. Vacca)

God mat och bra råvaror hör ihop. Med bra kött menar vi svenskt kött och det finns goda skäl till det. I Sverige får grisarna ha knorren kvar, korna får gå ute och beta på sommaren och djuren får halm och annat strö. I Sverige är djuren friskare än i många andra länder. Svenskt kött-märket betyder att 100 % av köttet i produkten är från gris, nöt, får eller lamm som är fött, uppfött, slaktat och styckat i Sverige. Hela produkten är tillverkad och förpackad i Sverige. Titta efter Svenskt kött-märket när du köper kött nästa gång!

Svenskt kött
svensktkott.se

SLAKTKROPP

ANATOMI

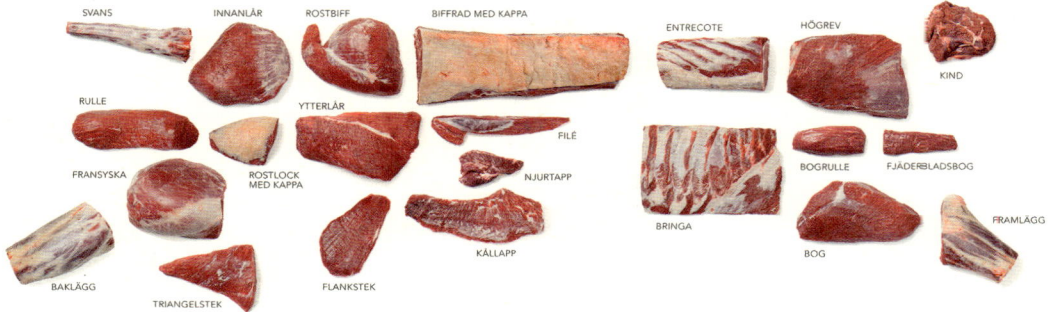

DETALJER

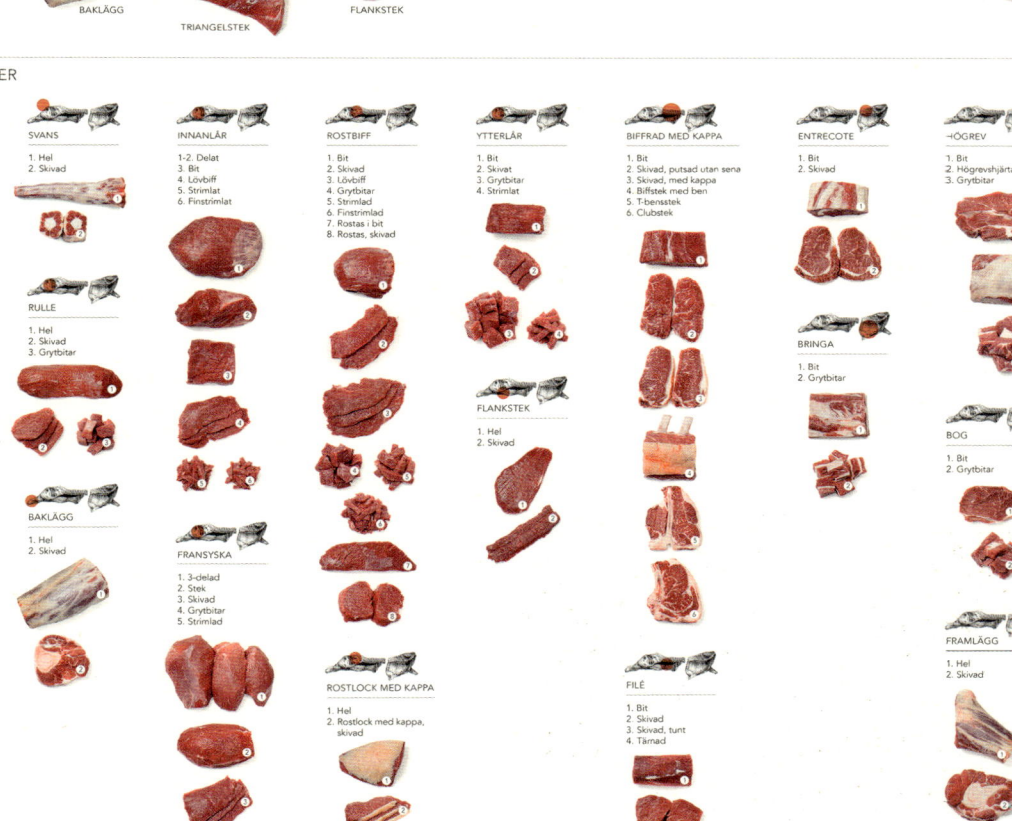

STUDIO · Between

DESIGN · Daniel Berglund, Thomas Åström

CITRUS MOON

In the packaging for this moon cake brand, the gradient green and yellow on the exterior cover represents the symbol of the mid-autumn full moon as well as the shape of a citrus fruit. The changing of lunar phases is revealed through the die-cut circle when the cover is being pulled off.

THE HARVEST OF THE MOON

Branding and packaging created for a new collection of Californian wine named "The Harvest of the Moon". The principal inspiration came from the visual characteristics of moon operation. The result is an iconic brand with strong recognition potential.

STUDIO · 8 Bis

DESIGN · Jean-Maxime Brais

GIUSEPPE GIUSSANI

Giuseppe Giussani is an Italian craftsman specialized in bespoke wood flooring. For his personal brand identity, the idea was to combine his name with tree ring patterns, symbolizing the craftsman's fate is tightly linked with wood.

Giuseppe Giussani
parquet d'artista

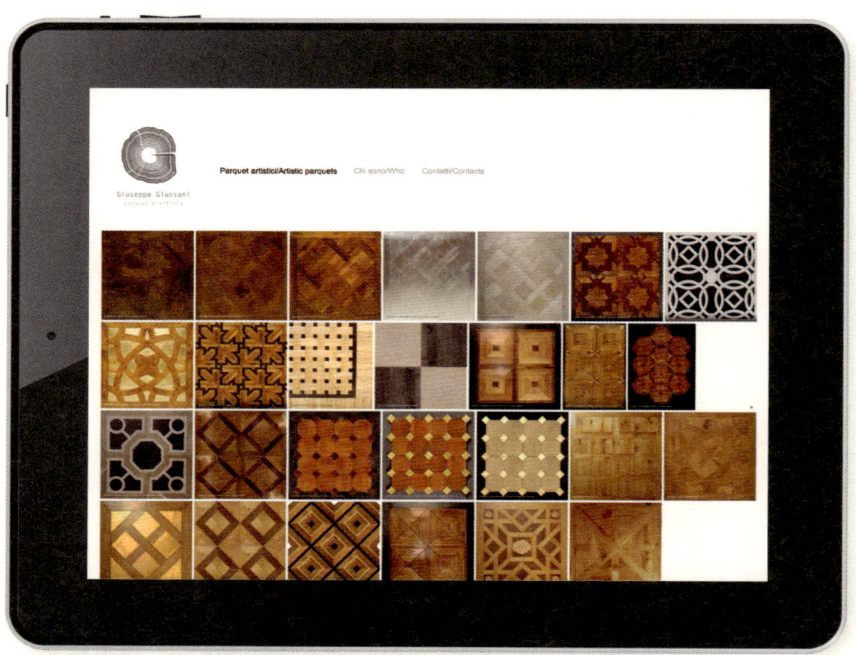

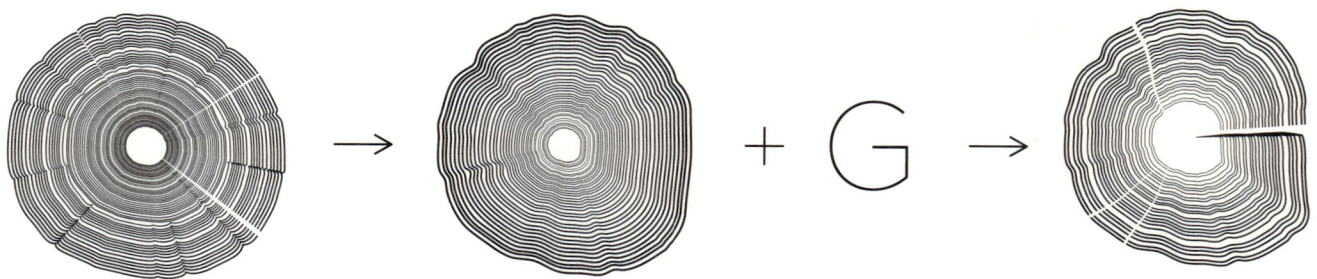

MÖBELBAU BREITENTHALER

"Möbelbau Breitenthaler" is an Austrian furniture brand known for its creative design, quality craftsmanship, and aesthetic appeal. The most symbolic element—a black and white wood ring-- was used in the brand identity to represent the timeless beauty the company was pursuing.

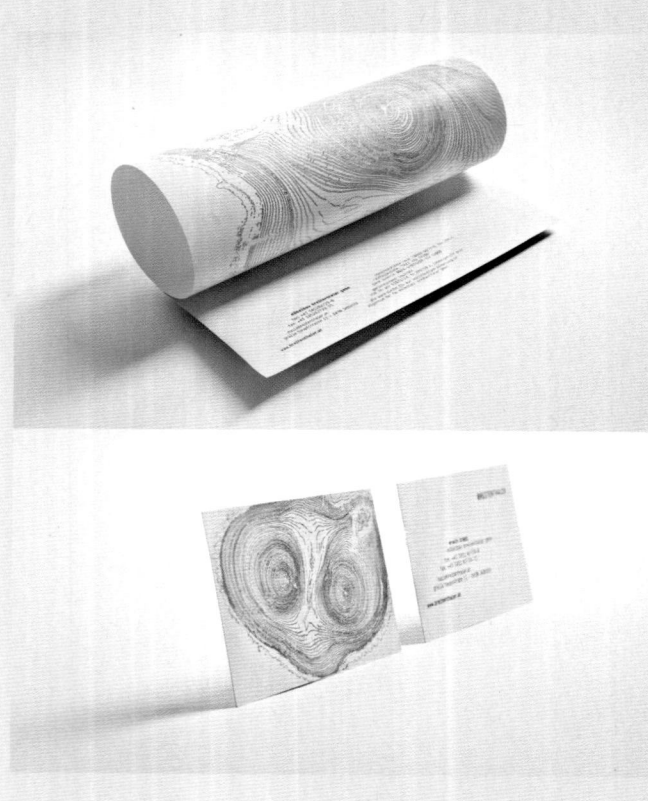

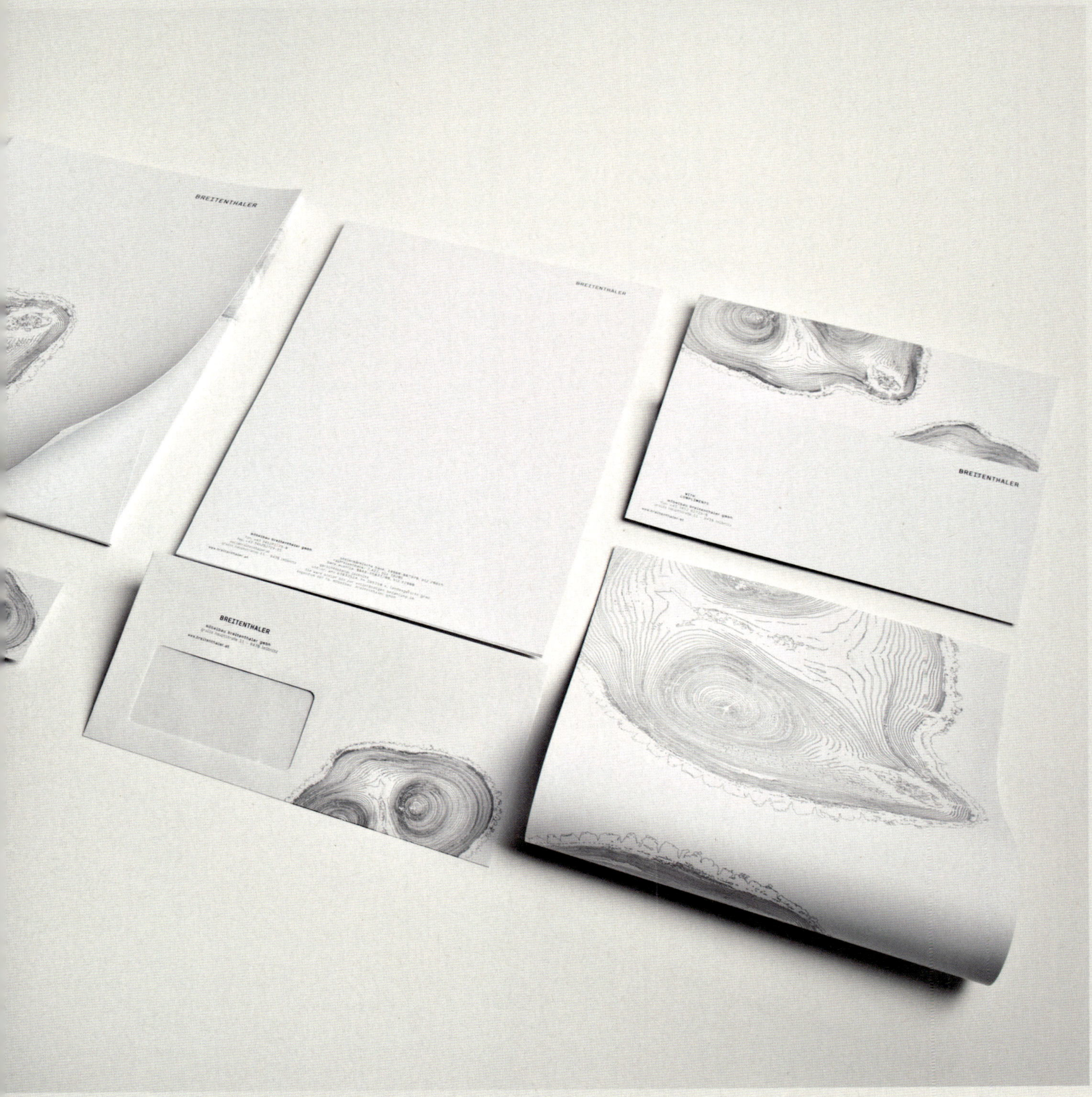

STUDIO · moodley brand identity

DESIGN · ALBERT HANDLER

INDEX

45gradi / P258
www.45gradi.com

6D / P180
www.6d-k.com

8 Bis / P256
www.8bisbranding.com

Ariadna Vilalta / P30
www.ariadnavilalta.com

Apartment One / P48
www.aptone.com

ACRE / P76 / P204
www.acre.sg

Anagrama / P66 / P108 / P160 / P200 / P224
www.anagrama.com

Antoniak / P72
www.antoniak.tk

Anton Starodubtcev / P114
www.behance.net/antsants

Artem Rulev / P152
www.behance.net/ArtemRulev

Alt Group / P220
www.altgroup.net

Artem Maslov / P234
www.art-maslov.ru

Atipus / P250
www.atipus.com

Bravo Company / P74
www.bravo-company.info

Booth / P106
www.wearebooth.com

Büro für Grafik Design / P198
www.raffaelstueken.de

Bessermachen DesignStudio / P214
www.bessermachen.com

BURO RENG / P242
www.buroreng.nl

Between / P252
www.between.se

Cody Petts / P92
www.codypetts.com

Cecilia Uhr / P144
www.ceciliauhr.co

Caroline Blanchette / P166
www.behance.net/carolineblanchette

Diana Gibadulina / P68
www.behance.net/dianagibadulina

DPZ Rio / P50
www.fernandaschmidt.com

Elizabeth Laferrière / P16
www.elizabethlaferriere.com

EPB / P26
www.espaciopacobascunan.com

E. Co., Ltd. / P52
www.e-ltd.co.jp

Ermolaev Bureau / P128
www.behance.net/ErmolaevBureau

Eskimo / P210
www.eskimodesign.ru

Elisa Ortiz / P248
www.behance.net/playingwithfoxes

EGGPLANT FACTORY / P112
www.eggplantfactory.co.kr

FONG QI WEI / P36
www.fqwimages.com

Fabio Persico Studio / P84
www.behance.net/fabiopersico

GBH / P20
www.gregorybonnerhale.com

gardenhada / P182
www.gardenhada.com

Giuseppe Fierro / P236
www.behance.net/giuseppefierro

Interabang / P32
www.interabang.uk.com

I&S BBDO / P46
www.isbbdo.co.jp

JWT BRAZIL / P60
www.jwt.com

Jesus Sotes / P118
www.jesussotes.com

Kasper Gram / P124
www.kaspergram.com

Karla Heredia Martínez / P134
www.behance.net/karlachic

Kevin Cantrell / P174
www.kevincantrell.com

KIAN brand agency / P190
www.kian.ru

Lumen Bigott / P142
www.lumenbigott.com

Lecter Johnson / P176
www.behance.net/lecter

MAMBO art & design studio / P80
www.bymambo.com

Mash / P102
www.mashdesign.com.au

ma7 / P130
www.behance.net/ma7

moo studio / P156
www.monikaostaszewska.com

Motherbird / P188
www.motherbird.com.au

Futura / P208
www.mfutura.mx

mousegraphics / P230
www.mousegraphics.gr

momonini creative space / P232
www.momonini.org

moodley brand identity / P260
www.moodley.at

Núria Vila / P212
www.nuriavila.net

Neue Design Studio / P226
www.neue.no

Orka Collective / P62
www.orkacollective.com

ORTOGRAFIKA / P148
www.ortografika.eu

Pure Living / P42
www.pureliving.ca

Pereira & O'Dell / P58
www.pereiraodell.com/

PJADAD / P64
www.pjadad.com

PND FUTURA / P78
www.photo.pndfutura.com

Plau Design / P140
www.plau.co

Polly Lindsay / P154
www.pollylindsay.com

Pedro Paulino / P178
www.pedropaulino.com

P576 / P202
www.p576.com

PRYSME / P240
www.prys.me

Raw Color / P70
www.rawcolor.nl

Russell Shaw Design / P82
www.russellshawblog.com

rsb designs / P146
www.notonthehighstreet.com/rsbdesigns

Remark Studio / P162
www.re-mark.co.uk

Robin L. Short / P164
www.cargocollective.com/robinshort

Ruslan Khasanov / P222
www.ruskhasanov.com

Seesaw / P34
www.seesawstudio.com.au

studio fnt / P122
www.studiofnt.com

Substance Limited / P126
www.substance.hk

Sarah Ouellet / P158
www.sarahouellet.com

Say What Studio / P170
www.saywhat-studio.com

Shanghai Starting 2000 / P184
www.starting2000.cn

Supafrank / P186
www.supafrank.com

Stockholm Design Lab / P216
www.stockholmdesignlab.se

The Clocksmiths / P14
www.theclocksmiths.it

TROONION Design / P24
www.trooniondesign.com

toormix / P56
www.toormix.com

Tracy Hung / P96
www.tracyhung.com

The Allotment Brand Design / P136
www.theallotmentbranddesign.com

Tamara Mihajlovic / P191
www.behance.net/TashMihajlovic

Thijs Biersteker / P238
www.thijsbiersteker.com

TSAN-YU YIN / P254
www.behance.net/tyyin

UNKA / P132
www.unka.cz

Victor Branding Design Corp / P104
www.victad.com.tw

Yana Basirova / P94
www.behance.net/basirrova

Ziggurat Brands / P54
www.zigguratbrands.com

Zé Studio / P246
www.ze-studio.com

Pick the sticker(s) you like to add a personal touch to the Nature Graphics cover.

ACKNOWLEDGEMENTS

We would like to thank all the designers and contributers who have been involved in the production of this book. Their significant contribution is indispensable in the compilation of this book. We would also like to express our gratitude to all the producers for their invaluable opinions and assistance throughout this project. And to the many others whose names are not credited but have made specific input in this book, we thank you for your continuous support.

FUTURE COOPERATIONS: If you wish to participate in SendPoints°Ø future projects and publications, please send your website or portfolio to editor01@sendpoints.cn